To
GEORGE & TIFI

YOUR 20TH ANNIVERS |

PLEASE INVITE ME TO YOUR 40TH!

Biblical

Marriage

OR
BETTER YET...

TO YOUR 50TH!!!

Yosef
MAY 25, 2012

MW00873093

Biblical Marriage

His plan for Courtship, Engagement, Wedding and Marriage

Joe Brusherd, a.k.a. *Yosef*

Self Published by Yosef
Rogers, AR

Biblical Marriage
His plan for courtship, Engagement, Wedding and Marriage

May be ordered through Amazon.com, Book store, Kindle or by contacting:

Yosef Brusherd
Yosef1@cox.net
www.InsightsByYosef.com
1-479-644-5262

ISBN: 13: 978-1477454473 (Eur.)
ISBN: 10: 1477454470 (U.S.A.)

Publish date: May 2012

Dedications

This book is dedicated to all the children
who will not have to cry themselves to sleep
because their parents' marriages have been saved or enriched

And

To all the children whose parents, step parent(s), grandparents
who will gain new understanding and develop
Godly relationships for their own sake
and for the sake of the children.

And

To the couples with blessed Marriages who will continue to be
a witness and testimony by living in accord with God's plan.

And

To my family who patiently helped me for over 50 years
of preparation to write this book

And

To a host of friends whose marriages have been a witness to me.

And

To my wife of 52 years who died March of 2012.
She now has a perfect husband.

CONTENTS

FOREWORD

We live in a modern world that is constantly changing and not necessarily for the better. The newer generations are losing the principals and values that God established for the family.

In this modern and changing world **BIBLICAL MARRIAGE** is a guide to help singles step by step on how to work toward forming a solid, biblical family with good moral values and utilizing biblical principles. For married couples **BIBLICAL MARRIAGE** is a helpful tool to restore their relationship to a biblical foundation and God's plan for their marriage.

Joe Brusherd, a.k.a. Yosef, supports his message utilizing biblical bases frequently enriched with illustrations of the Hebrew culture and customs. And his message is supported by the experience of over 50 years of marriage to his wife Peggy and the raising of six children who in turn are raising fourteen grandchildren, all serving the Lord.

The use of humorous and pointed testimonies and anecdotes makes **BIBLICAL MARRIAGE** a fun and enlightening book to read while providing solid biblical concepts and practical teachings that helps to establish a family according to God's plan.

By Miguel Carbajal,

Miguel and his wife Mayerling have developed a ministry to marriages while serving as pastors and missionaries.

PREFACE

Why did I want to write about Biblical Marriage?

Peggy and I were married for over 50 years, so this book is written by someone who has not only studied the topic but also lived through and experienced both the joy and the trials. Actually, after the initial joy, there seemed to be a lot of trials. Then in later years we have experienced the ultimate joy of seeing 14 grandchildren all growing in the love of the Lord.

You will find my personal background, testimony and credentials later in the *Author's Testimony*, but here I want to set forth the part of my background that provided motivation for writing this book. In the 30+ years that I have known Jesus as my Savior, Peggy and I have ministered to countless souls in their times of need, doubt and confusion. Without naming names, we have learned a lot about disconnects between God's plan for marriages and the direction the world is going. To jump to a conclusion, I am very concerned for future generations who are being raised in non-biblical ways – not according to the plan of our loving God, our Creator, who wants the best for His children.

My concern for the children of broken marriages came to light when our son shared a problem he encountered while leading a California church's youth group in 1983. He was simply teaching on 'God's love' when one student asked, "What is love?" Our son answered, "Well, it's kind of like the love your parents have for one another ..." The student interrupted and said "My parents are divorced. They hate each other." Our son then learned that less than 5% of school age children go home to both of their original parents. That encounter caused me to investigate further. I asked two teachers we knew at that time "How many of your students go home to their two original parents?" Both responded with very similar answers – "one or two in their class". And both teachers admitted that they were divorced and re-married and that they were also dealing with the 'his, hers and ours' issues in their own homes. By asking similar questions ever since, I have learned that the statistic may not be scientifically determined, but it is relatively correct and a serious problem in any case, including here in Arkansas – the so-called 'Bible belt'. Try discussing this problem with Christian teachers and watch the tears well up in their eyes.

Peggy and I have been blessed with seven children. One daughter died tragically at the age of ten months, so we have raised six children, two girls and four boys. In order to "accentuate the positive and eliminate the negative" I will not apologize for bragging on our children. In fact, a number of points are supported by testimonies from our children's lives – especially our baby daughter, Beth, and her marriage to Kirk, our favorite (and only) son-in-law. So this book will be salted with real testimonies. Those example testimonies that do not involve our children will remain anonymous for reasons that will sometimes be obvious.

How do we deal with Eastern vs. Western cultures?

Because I am and most readers will be products of Western culture this book will deal with and focus on our Western customs. Peggy and I have lived among, studied and encountered Eastern and European culture customs; and the application of these principles to Eastern culture is a logical extension of this study.[1] Some topics touch on the contrasting cultures; some relevant topics worthy of further consideration are (a) arranged marriages and (b) Monogamy or Polygamy.

Who will benefit from this book?

- Married couples – obviously;
- Singles planning to marry – obviously;
- Singles planning to remain single – ability to minister to and appreciate their married friends with children;
- Divorced/Separated – insights to avoiding pitfalls in future relationships and

---

[1] Authored "Hebraic Insights -- Messages Exploring the Hebrew Roots of Christian Faith", August 2011, based on our experience in a Messianic fellowship.

- Parents and ministers needing a background to minister to children involved in past separations.

This book asks many questions – to cause us think, to make memorable points, to encourage new trains of thought, to break us out of cultural boxes. Do you mind my asking questions?

Finally, we also believe that Marriage to His Son, Yeshua HaMashiach,[2] was and is and always will be God's end-times plan for all of us.

What is the communication style?

- Questions – This book asks many questions – to cause us to think, to make memorable points, to encourage new trains of thought, and to break us out of cultural boxes. Do you mind my asking questions? Do you mind that I do not try to answer all the questions? Is it possible that your answers would be better than mine?

- Humor – And I cannot help but slip in some humor to 'help the medicine go down'. And I happen to think Jesus used humor to keep twelve men and hundreds of disciples at His side while they listened to some tough teachings.

- Evangelistic – The sacrament of Marriage is a foreshadowing or a picture God's ultimate plan for us – to prepare the Church to be the bride at the "Wedding Supper of the Lamb".

- Testimonial – This is the best ways to learn, remember and illustrate points. People disagree with my preaching, and they argue with my teaching, but they cannot argue or disagree with my testimonies. They are truth and they are real.

All biblical references are from the New International Version, only because it seems to read smoothly.

---

[2] Yeshua HaMashiach is the Hebrew that has been translated to Greek and then to English as Jesus, the Christ. Literal translation is "Savior, the Messiah"

AUTHOR'S TESTIMONY

When Peggy and I married in 1959, our families almost laughed and thought the marriage will not last. How can marriage between a Catholic and a Methodist survive? The solution was easy for a few years – we didn't go to church.

But after seven children were born, one of which was killed as a child, faith in God became an issue. So Peggy and the older children accepted Jesus as their Savior. And years later, in 1976, Peggy and I experienced a 'marriage encounter' week-end in the Catholic Church. God stepped up his 'working on me'.

On August 25, 1977, I accepted Jesus at a Catholic Cursillo week-end when my knees buckled and I said loudly in my Spirit, "Jesus, you are real and I need to learn more about you." When I came home I found my whole family had been praying for me for ten years. On Sundays, Peggy and I enjoyed 'double-headers' -- both Catholic and Assembly of God churches as I had an insatiable hunger and thirst for God's Word.

Because we relocated a few times, we have been active in churches of diverse denominations – Baptist, Four Square Gospel, Word of Faith Charismatics, Filipino Assemblies, Assembly of God, and Messianic fellowships. Leadership roles included Sunday School teaching, Bible college courses, men's ministries, preaching and governance in each of the churches. Since 1982 I've served as president of four chapters of Full Gospel Business Men. The testimonies in countless 'men's ministry' meetings revealed a lot about successful and unsuccessful marriages and the biblical principles working or absent in marriages. After 20 years in California and Europe, we moved to Arkansas and found marriage issues in the 'Bible belt' were no different than the issues on the West coast.

While writing about Biblical Marriage, we were receiving an education in the Hebraic roots of our Christian faith in a Messianic fellowship which provided a rich understanding of the background of the times, culture and customs of marriage in biblical days. So let us study together to figure out why God gave the sacrament of marriage so much attention in His Word.

Yosef a.k.a. Joe Brusherd   May 2012

Chapter 1

The biblical basis for Marriage

Marriage is like twirling a baton,

turning handsprings or

eating with chopsticks.

It looks easy until you try to do it.

Now for the matters you wrote about: It is good for a man not to marry. But since there is so much immorality, <u>each man should have his own wife, and each woman her own husband.</u> The husband should fulfill his marital duty to his wife, and likewise the wife to her husband. The wife's body does not belong to her alone but also to her husband. In the same way, the husband's body does not belong to him alone but also to his wife. Do not deprive each other except by mutual consent and for a time, so that you may devote yourselves to prayer. Then come together again so that Satan will not tempt you because of your lack of self-control. I say this as a concession, not as a command.
1 Corinthians 7:1-7

The Bible is the basis for many of today's customs

In 1990 I was asked to substitute teach a Sunday school class. What made that request unique is that although I had been raised and saved in the Catholic Church, I was being asked to lead a classroom of the European contingent of missionaries and Bible college students and teachers at the main Assemblies of God church reaching out to Europe and Africa, including the Dean of the Bible college. God has a sense of humor. However, He also provides. The lesson dealt with the Wedding Supper of the Lamb – Revelation 19:9 *'Blessed are those who are invited to the wedding supper of the Lamb!'*

The Holy Spirit prompted me to ask the class for examples of modern day wedding customs. The entire session consisted of identifying today's wedding customs and relating each to a biblical story or message or principle. That discussion over 20 years ago initiated the hunger and thirst for this book. So, as a reader, be thinking about today's wedding traditions. Be looking for parallel examples in scripture and you will find many customs with scriptural foundation.

Why should we model our marriages on biblical principles?

The critical question! How important is it to enjoy a satisfying marriage here on earth with the joys and rewards He wants us to experience? Besides, you may not have to spend as much money on 'self-help' books!

Is getting to heaven and enjoying the marriage to The Bridegroom, Jesus, important to you? If yes, then this is a good time to practice being a good, faithful spouse?

We live in Today's Society/Culture. Our society is inundated from so many directions with sights, sounds, and activities, designed and destined to fracture the bulwark of marriage. Societal norms are changing and attempting to redefine what constitutes a marriage; 'entertainment' shows are glorifying extramarital activities -- each show more sordid than the last. For example, in the newspaper in 2005, *"Desperate Housewives"* and similar nominations were listed under the comedy category – have we now become so desensitized to this type of activity that it ceases to be sinful, and starts to be funny? Who are we kidding? In our sporting events at half-time – remember the 'clothing malfunction'? Consider the 'Ease Of Temptation' factor in today's world. Pornography is a 57 billion dollar Industry. To put this in perspective, 216 nations reported their Gross National Product. The pornography industry was larger than more than 169 of those 216 nations – meaning that only 47 nations had a higher GNP than the porn industry. The US Porn industry alone out produces the GNP of 132 of those 216 nations. Pornography searches account for some 68 million daily hits – 25% of all searches done on the internet are pornography related.

Here are more Sordid statistics:[3]

- Solicitations - 89% are made in youth chat rooms; 20% of the youth respond to them,
- Average age of first exposure – 11,
- Largest consumer group for porn – 12 to 17 year olds,
- Exposure - 80% of teens 15 to 17 years old report having multiple hard core exposure,
- Young people - 90% of 8 to 16 year olds have viewed porn, MOST while doing homework.
- Adults - 40 million regularly visit sites,
- Workplace - 20% of men and 13% of women admit to accessing pornography at work,
- Men - 53% of PROMISE KEEPER men viewed pornographic material at least once a week,
- Believers - 47% said pornography was a major problem in the home.

---

[3] While these statistics are outdated, similar information is available at www.familysafemedia.com/pornography_statistics.html

Is there any wonder that marriage is being attacked today? Is there any wonder that crimes of immorality are increasing?

This is not only an issue today, it was also an issues in Scripture. This is why Paul deals with the institution of marriage and the responsibilities of those who are married. The Bible declares that there is to be no sexual activity among those who are not married. Jesus was even more specific when He said in Matthew 5:28 *"But I tell you that anyone who looks at a woman lustfully has already committed adultery with her in his heart."* And in 1 Thessalonians 4:3 *It is God's will that you should be sanctified: that you should avoid sexual immorality.*

Greek society said sexual intimacy was OK, as long as you did not get tied down in marriage. That is why Paul had to point out to the Corinthians that the marital relationship is the deterrent to immorality. 1 Corinthians 7:2-5 *But since there is so much immorality, each man should have his own wife, and each woman her own husband. The husband should fulfill his marital duty to his wife, and likewise the wife to her husband. The wife's body does not belong to her alone but also to her husband. In the same way, the husband's body does not belong to him alone but also to his wife. Do not deprive each other...*

Scripture has a high view of marriage – Ephesians 5:22-23 *Wives, submit to your husbands as to the Lord. For the husband is the head of the wife as Christ is the head of the church, his body, of which he is the Savior.* The Bible first talks about marriage as a cleaving – a joining of the closest union possible. Marriage is a spiritual union on a physical plane, established by God alone -- Matthew 19:6 *"So they are no longer two, but one. Therefore, what God has joined together, let man not separate."*

I'm of the firm conviction that multiple wives were never God's intention. *And they will become one flesh* Gen. 2:24. The Hebraic Insight #75 – How Does God View Marriage,[4] was not intended to justify polygamy, but to focus on the responsibility of

---

[4] *"Hebraic Insights -- Messages Exploring the Hebrew Roots of Christian Faith"*, Insight #75, August 2011 by Yosef Brusherd

the virgin to save her virginity for the wedding day. To this day, the Jewish custom is for families to promise virginity in the ketubah, marriage contract, and for the couple to come forth with the evidence. This is admittedly more difficult in practice and in our current culture, but what we are seeking is to understand how we should follow the ideal that God Himself specified and Yeshua supported.

What jeopardizes the definition & purpose of marriage?

Today, the social, legal and religious communities are allowing the God ordained foundational roles of male and female to be altered, confused and sometimes switched. Let this book deal with the way life should be, rather than building a case for the numerous ways our culture is changing to satisfy selfish desires of man. Man should be honoring God's commandments, instructions, and rules for being blessed, instead of disobeying or ignoring and therefore being cursed.

What would happen to the market for 'self-help' books if we had sound marriages? If I may answer a question with a question – would sound marriages eliminate the need for most 'self-help' books? Most topics in those books deal with issues that would not even exist if biblical principles were applied to the marriages. But, first ...

How do we deal with Eastern vs. Western cultures? Because I am, and most readers will be, products of Western culture, this book will deal with and focus on our Western customs. Peggy and I have lived among, studied, and encountered Eastern culture customs; and the application of these principles to Eastern culture is a logical extension of this study. So, topics relevant and worthy of further consideration are

(a) Arranged marriages -- will be referenced to some degree in the Courting and Engagement chapters.

(b) Monogamy or Polygamy. This raises challenging questions – Old Testament, Eastern cultures and some current customs practice polygamy even today. And there is a concern that our Western culture is practicing polygamy – serially instead of in parallel. The real question here is - which method has the most negative impact on all the parties involved? Don't let this question distract you from appreciating God's original plan as clarified by the apostle Paul. He gave advise to both Timothy and Titus regarding appropriate leadership examples. i.e. Titus 1:6 *An elder must be blameless, the husband of but one wife, ..*

What are the steps to achieving a sound marriage?

The biblical process toward a sound marriage consist of a step-wise biblical discipline of (1st) courtship, (2nd) engagement/betrothal, (3rd) wedding, (4th) marriage. This book analyzes each of these four macro steps; demonstrating the importance of each in leading to sound marriages.

Unfortunately, we all pick up this information when we have already found ourselves somewhere in the midst of the process having made a few, if not many, mistakes already. That's understandable and the Lord is ready to pick us up where we are and guide us on the path going forward. Remember, we serve a forward looking Savior, not a backward reminder like Satan.

Unfortunately, most children, while still children, have probably not been coached on the definition of love and healthy relationships. Parents don't tend to have those talks with their children. At least this topic is touched on in churches, if the child is fortunate to be among the minority that attends a church with a good Sunday school program. As important, if not more important, is Sex Education which is not taught in church. Parents tend to do a very awkward job of describing sex in a positive light.

An excellent book on Sex Education is *"Almost Twelve"* by Kenneth Taylor. He wrote the *"Living Bible"* and he also wrote *"Almost Twelve"* with a sense that God created sex for good purposes and it is a gift to be treasured. Here is the author's marketing blurb: *It seems as if the whole world is talking and singing about sex. Sex is discussed in health class, and some kids talk about it at school and even tell dirty jokes to make their friends laugh. What's a parent to do? 'Almost 12'[5] is a book for Christian kids and others who want to know what God has to say about sex so they can do what is right and can please Him.* There would be a lot fewer sex related mistakes by young people if all parents sat and read this book, cover to cover, with their child, and ideally shoulder to shoulder. I've done it. It works.

Are there misconceptions re man and woman, husband and wife?

The Bible (OT & NT for the most part) was translated into Greek and then into English. Thus some Greek philosophy crept into the translation process resulting in a degradation of the role of women and wives. Greek philosophy depicted women as the lesser, destined to stay at home and to stop thinking. Other cultures of the time did not support or practice that denigration of women, but the Bible was translated through Greek thought-life.

To set the record straight, let us take a fresh look at the story of creation in Genesis. Women have been accused of being the weaker sex because Eve fell for the lies of the serpent. Unfortunately, three other equally plausible interpretations seem to have been overlooked and are worth considering before we let 'traditional thinking' warp our understanding of biblical marriage. Consider these three alternative interpretations:

1. Why did the serpent wait until he could tempt Eve? Instead of assuming that Eve, as a woman, was the weaker and most vulnerable, could it be that the intended role of

---

[5] Taylor, Kenneth N. *Almost 12: The Story of Sex*. 3rd ed. Wheaton, IL: Tyndale House, 1995.

husbands and wives was to provide each other with moral support. When the serpent caught either one alone, then the support system fails, sin enters in and corrupts the relationship.

2. Did the serpent deliberately select Eve because she was weaker, more vulnerable? Or could it be the tempter felt that Eve, as a woman, represented the stronger of the two? To take down an opponent, why not disarm the stronger one. Consider that the serpent had to argue rather skillfully to lead Eve astray; then she simply handed the fruit to Adam and that was sufficient to lead him astray. Who was stronger in this view?

3. Another consideration, Satan was banished to earth and this was his dominion. Now God Almighty placed his awesome creation – man and woman created in His likeness – into Satan's territory. Maybe Satan wanted to start a civil war within that sacred union as Satan still wants to do to this day.

Study of the original Hebrew in the famous passage that says God created Eve out of the side or from a rib of Adam. The Hebrew word used in Genesis 2:20 to describe "help meet" is *neged* (Hebrew) which implies "opposing."[6] Here is the symbolic definition of the Hebrew characters: "*the door to helper providing life.*" Men, does that describe your wife?

The opposing aspect seems contrary to the harmonious relationships being advertised for today's Internet couplings. But consider what the Irish singer Bono said: "*I would be terrified to be on my own as a solo singer. I surround myself with ... a band, a family of very spunky kids, and a wife who's smarter than anyone ... you're only as good as*

---

[6] Strong's Hebrew Definition OT:5046—properly, to front, i.e. stand boldly out opposite; by implication (causatively), to manifest; figuratively, to announce (always by word of mouth to one present); specifically, to expose, predict, explain, praise.

the argument you get." And Proverbs 27:17 says, *As iron sharpens iron, so one man sharpens another* (NIV).

When we studied this in a recent Bible study and viewed our four families around the table, we were impressed with the contrasting characters of our respective spouses *that God gave us.* Now we know why he chose us for each other!

Point to ponder

If you don't think like your spouse does,
could that have been God's intention?

Why do we need a four step process of -- Courtship, Engagement, Wedding, Marriage?

Now we will research Biblical Marriage by going through the traditional, chronological process –

(1st) falling in love and courting,

(2nd) getting engaged or betrothed,

(3rd) wedding,

(4th) marriage.

If everyone had proceeded, or does proceed, toward Marriage by using God's scriptural principles, the world would be a better place.

So let us cover the four step process chapter by chapter identifying biblical principles, so we can avoid the pitfalls that Satan, and our flesh, put in our paths.

Chapter 2

Falling in Love and Courting

**He who finds a wife finds what is good and
receives favor from the LORD.** Prov.18:22

Who is the implied pursuer in this Proverb? He? or She?

---

*With Tongue in cheek, let us look at Hollywood's Formula leading to
deep, intimate, sizzling relationships that one hopes will last forever.*
    Step 1. Find the right person –
                  be on the lookout. He/She is out there.
    Step 2. Fall in Love –
                  you'll just know by the chemistry – first date!
    Step 3. Fix All Your Hopes & Dreams –
                  on him/her for your future fulfillment
    Step 4. When Failure Happens –
                  Repeat Steps 1, 2 and 3

---

*It has been said that "Falling in love" produces some of the most wonderful and
powerful emotions we can experience, while simultaneously warping our ability
to think clearly. If you are over 21 years of age, you can probably relate.*

Who is the pursuer and who is the pursued?

Our son-in-law, Kirk, demonstrated this principle very early in his relationship with our daughter, Beth. They were attending the same church, but Beth was dating someone else when Kirk first approached her with a question – "Beth, will you please let me know when I may court you?" When Beth told us that, as her father, I knew there was something right and special about that young man. He was clearly the pursuer and she was to be the 'pursuee'. And he wanted to go about the process respectfully.

However, the example that awakened me to the importance of this principle in courtship was a statement made by a Christian woman who was licking her wounds after her third divorce. Her comment was "I sure have done a poor job of picking husbands."

Whoa!   Who was pursuing who?

Proverbs 18:22 *He who finds a wife finds what is good and receives favor from the LORD.* Biblically, 'he' is being advised that 'he' is to find a good wife -   Incidentally, Proverbs 31 is known for its 'Godly wife' explanation starting in verse 10. Upon closer examination you will find that the whole of Proverbs chapter 31 starting in verse 1 is a mother's advice to her son, King Lemuel (Bathsheba's nickname for Solomon). Now if the King's mother thought it was important for her son to select his wife carefully, maybe we have something to learn. And she assumed that 'he' was to find and select 'her'.

Biblical principles are also practical. The underlying dynamics need to be understood in a practical sense. If 'he' is the pursuer, then there is commitment. If 'she' is the pursuer, he may consent out of a heavier dose of 'lust' than 'love'. Enough said, especially dealing with the typical dating that leads to marriage age of teens and early twenties. Was advice sought from parents, pastors or mature elders?

A young, or older, man ought to be very concerned when he finds that she is chasing him. What are her motives? How might I find myself hooked? How is she trying to hook me? Where might this lead? What would God say about this relationship? Can He, Our LORD, go with us on our dates?

Another testimony – When I first presented this outline as a teaching at a Wednesday Night Service, the pursuer/pursuee topic was the opening point. I noticed the Pastor deliberately caught the eye of his widowed secretary in a very knowing way. Just before the teaching she had prayed for her 600 mile trip to meet a man who she was hoping would be the 'new love of her life'. So both the Pastor and I knew that the eye contact meant to raise the question – "who was pursuing who?" Peggy and I attended her wedding. The marriage was very short term.

What should be the criteria for selecting a bride, a wife?

Doesn't it make sense to pre-plan something that is a lifetime commitment? So, shouldn't there be criteria for selecting a bride/wife? Abraham's servant (typology of the Holy Spirit thought so. Genesis 24:10-21 -- *Then the servant took ten of his master's camels and left ... He had the camels kneel down near the well outside the town; ... Then he prayed, "O LORD, ... May it be that when I say to a girl, 'Please let down your jar that I may have a drink,' and she says, 'Drink, and I'll water your camels too' — let her be the one you have chosen for your servant Isaac. By this I will know that you have shown kindness to my master."*

(He established Criteria ... and God answered his prayer)

15 Before he had finished praying, Rebekah came out with her jar on her shoulder. She was the daughter of Bethuel son of Milcah, who was the wife of Abraham's brother Nahor. The girl was very beautiful, a virgin; no man had ever lain with her. She went down to the spring, filled her jar and came up again. The servant hurried to meet her and said, "Please give me a little water from your jar." "Drink, my lord," she said, and quickly lowered the jar to her hands and gave him a drink. After she had given him a drink, she said, "I'll draw water for your camels too, until they have finished drinking." So she quickly emptied her jar into the trough, ran back to the well to draw more water, and drew enough for all his camels. Without saying a word, the man watched her closely to learn whether or not the LORD had made his journey successful.

She qualified, based on the criteria the Servant established.

This biblical example deals with the procuring of a wife for Isaac. We will parse the passage in greater detail in the next chapter on Engagement/Betrothal.

Let me present for your consideration three CRITERIA SUGGESTIONS that I have been sharing with young men, in order to get their attention:

1. Don't date a girl you wouldn't marry. This first one came from my sons, who came home from Christian colleges with this admonition drilled into them. It also reminds me of the traditional Jewish mother that told her daughter "You do not have to marry a doctor... Just hang around with them".

2. Make sure the sparkle in her eye isn't the light shining through from the other side. This second criteria came from my mother. Hopefully, no explanation is required.

3. Pick your wife with your ears, not your eyes. This is the most important criteria in my opinion (based on 50+ years of marriage). Unfortunately when sharing the third criteria with groups, the younger men downplay or refuse to acknowledge the importance of this advice. If you have been married more than five years, what do you have to say about the importance of the this third criteria? And our goal is to celebrate at least a silver anniversary. How many years of listening does that require? Especially when she has the proverbial 10,000 words a day to get out, compared with his 3,000 words.

The first criteria is a given. The remainder of this section on Dating and Courting will assume the purpose is to eventually find the appropriate partner for life – a wife. Any other dating or courting or meeting activity is fraught with dangers, pitfalls and/or leads toward sinful behavior. Do I need to repeat this last thought?

What does the Bible say about selecting a bride, a wife?

The typical admonition regarding partner selection is the oft-quoted 2 Corinthians 6:14-16 *Do not be yoked together with unbelievers. For what do righteousness and wickedness have in common? Or what fellowship can light have with darkness? What harmony is there between Christ and Belial? What does a believer have in common with an unbeliever? What agreement is there between the temple of God and idols?* That is one and the same message repeated by re-wording six times. The Holy Spirit and Paul must have both thought it to be important!

Notice that this scriptural reference is stated as a clear and direct 'command', not simply 'advice'. All too often the first 6 words are stated as advice, without the full impact of the reasoning that follows in context. Even Solomon, the wisest man ever, was brought down by 'foreign wives'; and future generations suffered as a result. A study of the book of 1 Kings reveals a series of corrupted Kings influenced by 'foreign wives'.

Arranged marriages are still common elsewhere in the world as well as in the biblical times and in Eastern culture. But here in the Western culture we honor and worship 'independence'. Doesn't commandment number five say we should give honor to parents? Hmmm! Is it possible that parents and elderly folks may have reasoning worth listening to?

Q- Why did God give older folks grey hair?

A – So younger folks would know who to go to with questions about life.

A classic biblical example of partner selection comes from the Old Testament. Abraham was trying to protect the bloodline and be worthy of the blessings of God for his family and for all of us who have sung "Father Abraham had many sons, many sons had father Abraham ...". Genesis 24:1-4 *Abraham ... said to the chief servant ... I want you to swear by the LORD ... that you will not get a wife for my son from the daughters of the Canaanites, among whom I am living, but will go to my country and my own relatives and get a wife for my son Isaac."*

Abraham wanted the best for his son; he did not want his son to marry outside of the 'bloodline'. We too have a bloodline to protect – the blood of Jesus, shed so we could be members of the 'family of God'. Abraham's reasoning was valid and his heart was for his child's best interest. He wanted his son to be 'equally yoked'.

> Whenever God gives us a command, it is <u>always</u> for our own good. Every command from a parent is for the good of his/her child.

Can we learn and listen to a lesson from this example? Parents have the best interests of their children in mind when they try to arrange marriages. In cultures where respect for family and parents is high, arranged marriages become the norm. What has happened to the fifth commandment? Exodus 20:12 *Honor your father and your mother, so that you may live long in the land the LORD your God is giving you.* Do we question the definition of 'honor' or do we think there is a time/age limit on this commandment? And don't limit the definition of the word 'land'!

The example of Abraham's concern for his son's marriage is also interpreted by the church as a typology of the operation of the triune Godhead in carrying out Their plan of salvation. Abraham (Father) sends His Servant (Holy Spirit) to find a bride for his Isaac (Jesus) from among His people (us here on earth).

We have another example of a marriage being arranged in the classic case of Joseph and Mary. God the Father arranged for two hand-picked or God-chosen people to be the earthly parents for the Son of God. Without retelling the Christmas story, we have heard many explanations of what Joseph and Mary faced as individuals dealing with a very counter-cultural phenomenon.

Are we a product of an arranged marriage already? Did you choose God? Or did He choose you?

Maybe arranged marriages are a good thing after all!

HOWEVER, for arranged marriages to work today requires a cultural support system. In our Western culture, divorce is so prevalent that either party of the arranged marriage could too easily slip out and there is limited or little social retribution. Not so in

Eastern culture (if I may define the two cultures so simply). And also ponder the problem of the divorce rate in the Evangelical Christian Churches being comparable to the divorce rate in the 'world'.

Point to ponder

In what ways does our 'Western culture' cause arranged marriages to be unworkable?

And is that a good thing?

"Western culture!" Is that an oxymoron?

Arranged marriages; do parents have a role in the selection?

First, God tells us to. We have typical advice from the Old Testament in Jeremiah 29:5-6 *Marry and have sons and daughters; find wives for your sons and give your daughters in marriage, so that they too may have sons and daughters.* Parents, you are picking the mother of your grandchildren! Or you are giving your daughter to the father of your grandchildren.

Joseph was submitted to Pharaoh and in Genesis 41:45 -- *Pharaoh gave Joseph the name Zaphenath-Paneah and gave him Asenath daughter of Potiphera, priest of On, to be his wife.* We'll have much more to say later.

Who hasn't heard of 'match-making mothers'? I have a lot of respect for the underlying respect that Jews have for God's laws. One of my favorite movies is "Fiddler on the Roof" in which Tevye is dealing with three daughters going around the traditions of using a 'match-maker'.

Who is better equipped to select the right bride for a son? A 19 year-old young man who is still learning what it is to be a man. Or parents who have had 'umpteen' years of marital experience?

Specifically, a 19 year-old woman has been observing and talking to peers and processing inter-personal relationships as-well-as babysitting and house-keeping responsibilities. That results in a maturity level that is not matched by a 19 year old young man whose God-given hormonal drive is at its peak.

While we are on the topic of 'arranged marriages', let us consider that in cultures, biblical and others, where 'match-making' is the norm, the culture embraces the arrangement. Divorce is not an option. Becoming one in the flesh is the community's expectation. Obedience to the tradition and the family honor are respected and treasured. Therefore it works better in those environments. Sorry to say that in today's Western culture, the environment, and even the Christian influence is insufficient to sustain an enduring marriage.

Are there biblical examples of WRONG ways to find a wife?

What happens when the young man selects his own bride?

Samson's choices serve as a biblical example of what not to do. Judges 14:1-3 *Samson went down to Timnah and saw there a young Philistine woman. When he returned, he said to his father and mother, "I have seen a Philistine woman in Timnah; now get her for me as my wife." His father and mother replied, "Isn't there an acceptable woman among your relatives or among all our people? Must you go to the uncircumcised Philistines to get a wife?" But Samson said to his father, "Get her for me. She's the right one for me."*

Clearly, Samson was headstrong, spoiled and not seeking or honoring advice. His decision was clearly counter-custom. He disregarded the fifth commandment. As a result, that marriage was a disaster that caused the loss of many lives.

Samson was also guilty of seeking out a 'mixed marriage'. You know the kind – 'unequally yoked' as we traditionally call that relationship. Since the wedding feast lasted seven days with the two families celebrating together, what kind of pressures did that create with familial relationships? There is no way that couple's relationship could get off on the right foot. In today's culture, how well can an 'unequally yoked' couple deal with questions like:

        a) which Church to attend?
        b) how to raise children?
        c) where to spend holidays?
        d) what is the criteria for language in the household?
        e) etc.

Through Esau's rebellious attitude and actions God provides us with another example. Genesis 28:8-9 *Esau then realized how displeasing the Canaanite women were to his father Isaac; so he went to Ishmael and married Mahalath, the sister of Nebaioth and daughter of Ishmael son of Abraham, in addition to the wives he already had.* He married out of rebellion which only created enmity between his people, the Edomites, (enemies of God) and the Israelites (God's chosen). And today we are still living with damaged relationship between the Jews and their neighbors as a result.

We are all too familiar with the damage done by marriages which were performed without the blessing of the parents.

Should he pray for wisdom or guidance to court the right girl?

How many single girls pray to be courted by a Godly man, or by God's choice? Conversely, young single men should also be praying. When Abraham's servant was searching for the right wife for Isaac, he prayed a prayer that could be an example.

Genesis 24:12-15 *Then he prayed, "O LORD, ... , give me success today, and show kindness to my master Abraham... . the daughters of the townspeople are coming out to draw water. May it be that when I say to a girl, 'Please let down your jar that I may have a drink,' and she says, 'Drink, and I'll water your camels too' — let her be the one you have chosen for your servant Isaac. By this I will know that you have shown kindness to my master." Before he had finished praying, Rebekah came* ...

Do you believe that God wants to answer that prayer? His way? By providing the right life partner for you?

What is the courting process?

Simple things like:

- 'He' goes to her house to pick 'her' up for their dates.

- 'He' customarily goes up to 'her' door and knocks. I know it is a fading custom. So, if he sits in the car and blows the horn, don't come out. Beware! Don't ever come out!

- *"He came from heaven to earth, to show the way ..."* as the popular song reflects Jesus' own words in John 6:41 where Jesus said *"I am the bread that came down from heaven."*

For biblical examples let's start with Abraham and his servant.
Continuing with Genesis 24:10 *Then the servant took ten of his master's camels and left, taking with him all kinds of good things from his master. He set out for Aram Naharaim and made his way to the town of Nahor.* The search went to 'her' house, not expecting 'her' to come to 'him'.

How did Jesus knock on the door of the Samaritan woman at the well? Jesus initiated the conversation with the woman at the well. John 4:7 *When a Samaritan woman came to draw water, Jesus said to her, "Will you give me a drink?"* How did Jesus knock on her door? Who started the conversation?

Who does the door knocking in these popular verses?

- Revelation 3:11 *"I am coming soon. Hold on to what you have, so that no one will take your crown."*

- And again in Revelation 3:20 *"Here I am! I stand at the door and knock. If anyone hears my voice and opens the door, I will come in ..."*

How do you distinguish between love and lust?

Since we assume all readers are mature enough to understand 'lust', let us simply focus on the ideal – 'love'.

Apostle John reminded us of Jesus' ultimate act of love in John 12:32 "*to be lifted up to draw all men unto me*".

And Isaiah said it well in Isaiah 62:5 - "*as a bridegroom rejoices over his bride, so will your God rejoice over you.*"

One of the most important statements in the Bible, especially recognized by the Israelite children is known in Hebrew as "Shema" (Hear) Deuteronomy 6:4-5 <u>Hear</u>, *O Israel: The LORD our God, the LORD is one. 5 Love the LORD your God with all your heart and with all your soul and with all your strength.* Love the Lord your God with all your heart. Love for the Groom. If you have not figured it out yet, know that our key theme in this book is that Jesus is our Bridegroom and we are looking forward to consummating a marriage with Him.

Even the apostle John remembered Peter's words when writing the gospel message in John 21:15 *"Yes, Lord," he (Peter) said, "you know that I love you."*

Remember that love song?

♪ **"*Getting to know you, getting to know all about you.*"** ♪

And there is a line in a modern hymn describing our relationship with Jesus "*I want to know you more.*" It should be part of the courting process to be searching to know each other well. Likes, dislikes, future plans, family backgrounds that will impact life-styles and daily-habits, religious beliefs and life's purpose and goals.

As the future bride of Christ, we are taught in Psalm 139:23-24 to ask Him to *Search me, O God, and know my heart; test me and know my anxious thoughts. 24 See if there is any offensive way in me, and lead me in the way everlasting.*

And in turn, our Bridegroom is searching deep into our hearts, since we are his future bride. See Jeremiah 17:10 *"I the LORD search the heart and examine the mind, ..."*

Yes, we are challenged in 2 Corinthians 13:5 to examine our relationship with Him – e*xamine yourselves to see whether you are in the faith; test yourselves. Do you not realize that Christ Jesus is in you - unless, of course, you fail the test?* We the bride want to learn more about the groom - studying, asking questions, finding things in common, asking the tough questions! How many marriages would be stronger, or salvaged, if the tough questions were asked during courtship?

Point to Ponder

Are you being courted by Jesus Christ?

How important is 'Romance'?

Romance is obviously important, almost unavoidable and romance is the fun part of courtship. Here are some dictionary definitions that reflect the excitement surrounding 'Romance':

- A love affair.
- Ardent emotional attachment or involvement between people; love: *They kept the romance alive in their marriage for 35 years.*
- A strong, sometimes short-lived attachment, fascination, or enthusiasm for something: *a childhood romance with the sea.*
- A mysterious or fascinating quality or appeal, as of something adventurous, heroic, or strangely beautiful:

Sometimes 'romance' is demonstrated by acts of kindness, like when Jacob was pursuing Rachel in Genesis 29:10-11 *When Jacob saw Rachel daughter of Laban, his mother's brother, and Laban's sheep, he went over and rolled the stone away from the mouth of the well and watered his uncle's sheep. Then Jacob kissed Rachel and began to weep aloud.* Don't you get thrilled hearing stories of 'love at first sight'?

Do you have love for your Bridegroom-to-be?

Moses recognized God's love for His people after the exodus across the Red Sea. Moses acknowledged God's love in song in Exodus 15:13? *"In your (God's) unfailing love you will lead the people you have redeemed."*

Points to ponder

Have you met Jesus?

How or when did you first meet Him?

Was it love at first sight?

Is it a romantic relationship?

Are you enjoying getting to know Him?

What is friendship at a higher level?[7]

What is unique about the friendship between Jonathan and David? What can we learn from it?

It was a unique love in that it was destined to endure forever. Neither David nor Jonathan received any gain or profit from their relationship; neither had any ulterior motive. Their friendship was entirely genuine and selfless and as such serves as the biblical paradigm of the ideal relationship. In fact, Jonathan was eligible to be and was the likely heir to his father Saul's throne; David was the new kid on the block emerging as the military hero and thus, the competitor for the future kingship which Jonathan

---

[7] Excerpts from Hebraic Musing e-mail published by Yosef, April 10, 2012

had expected to receive. Jonathan would have naturally joined in his father's desire to rid the kingdom of David because of the threat posed by David. But we read 1 Sam. 18:3-4 *Then Jonathan and David made a covenant because he loved him as his own soul. And Jonathan took off the robe that was on him and gave it to David, with his armor, even to his sword and his bow and his belt.* NJKV

A poignant, entertaining, pithy, short Rabbinical Jewish work, *Ethics of the Fathers,* teaches "*Any love that is dependent on an external factor, when that factor is removed, the love fades away; while love that is not dependent on anything will endure forever; this is the love between David and Jonathan.*" This brings 'friendship' to a higher level.

Points to ponder

How many of our friends do we call a "friend" because we receive something from the relationship?

Who arranged our relationship with Him?

No study of love would be complete without referencing John 3:16 *"For God so loved the world that he gave his one and only Son, that whoever believes in him shall not perish but have eternal life.*

Jesus, the groom-to-be was given by the Father, came to us, His bride-to-be. He pursued and is still pursuing us with the help of the 'helper', the Holy Spirit. Here are a few 'choice' examples:

- John 15:16 *You did not choose me, but I chose you ...*

- 1 Corinthians 1:27-28 *But God chose the foolish things of the world to shame the wise; God chose the weak things of the world to shame the strong. He chose the lowly things of this world ...*

- 2 Thessalonians 2:13 *from the beginning God chose you ...*

- James 1:18 *He chose to give us birth through the word of truth, that we might be a kind of firstfruits of all he created.*

- Ephesians.5:22 *Wives, submit to your husbands as to the Lord.*

- Ephesians 1:4-5 *For he chose us in him before the creation of the world to be holy and blameless in his sight. In love he predestined us to be adopted as his <u>sons</u> through Jesus Christ,* ... (an arranged marriage! By the Father)

Point to Ponder

God calls us 'sons'... but as brides of the Son, aren't we 'daughters-in-law'?

So what is the next step?

So we are in love, getting to know one another and wanting to get married. We (or someone) decided we want to spend the rest of our lives together. What is the next step?

But, to be realistic, before going to the next step, we need to discuss the role of sex in this relationship building process. Somewhere in this process the urge, draw, activity, actions, complications, temptations, of the sex issue have been stirred up. Let me share excerpts from *Hebraic Insight #76 – Is Sex Good or Bad?*[8]

Hebraic Insight #76 – Is Sex Good or Bad? excerpt

We have been raised with a puritanical attitude toward the topic of, or anything to do with, sex. Within Christianity, the holiness movement has been so protective of dress codes that might stir the imagination that sex has been driven out of our education system and out of church teaching. So when the schools or the guys at the firehouse teach sex, it is in a red-faced and embarrassing mode. Maybe I am overstating the situation somewhat, but on the other

---

[8] *"Hebraic Insights -- Messages Exploring the Hebrew Roots of Christian Faith"*, Insight chapter #76, August 2011 by Yosef Brusherd

hand, when we treat the topic as forbidden or bad or something you should not do or even think about, we are causing curiosity, experimentation and boundary challenging. ...

The Bible clearly distinguishes male and female in many ways and for many purposes. God created sex, so it must be good. We would not be here if it were not for sex. God's first commandment was in Genesis 1:27–28: *Male and female he created them. God blessed them: God said to them, "Be fruitful, multiply, fill the earth and subdue it"* (CJB).

Let's answer the key question, is sex good or bad? In the Torah study group I answered the question with a question: "Is the fire in the fireplace good?" Naturally the answer was yes. Next question: "When there is a fire outside of the fireplace, is that good or bad?" Everyone cringed as we each visualized the damage and devastation caused by fire out of control and in the wrong or unintended place. It is the same with sex. When it is where it belongs and for the right purpose, it is great and we can thank God for giving us this gift. However, when sex is not where God intended it to be, it wreaks havoc. We can all visualize the damage we have seen, heard, or experienced, caused by infidelity, fornication, premarital sex, and adultery and the resultant desolation of marriages, families, and relationships. These damaged relationships are top priorities to God.

Falling in Love and Courting

Chapter 3

The Engagement or Betrothal

a contract; an agreement; a covenant relationship

Abraham wants to find a wife for his precious son Isaac.
Let's read this classic betrothal story carefully and enjoy it!

Story of Abraham & his Servant & Isaac & Rebekah

How many customs were described in the courting and marriage story of Isaac and Rebekah in Genesis 24:1-56? [9] Comments in parenthesis are added to illustrate principles to be discussed later. How many customs can you identify?

The groom goes to the bride's house: *Abraham ... said to the chief servant in his household* [Holy Spirit?], *"I want you to swear by the LORD ... that you will not get a wife for my son from the daughters of the Canaanites, among whom I am living* [don't be unequally yoked], *but will go to my country and my own relatives and get a wife for my son Isaac"* [an arranged marriage] ...

The selection criteria: *Then the servant took ten of his master's camels and left, taking with him all kinds of good things from his master* [gifts for her]. *He set out for ... the town of Nahor. He had the camels kneel down near the well outside the town; it was toward evening, the time the women go out to draw water* [courting at the watering hole sounds familiar]. *Then he prayed, "O Lord, God of my master Abraham, give me success today, and show kindness to my master Abraham. See, I am standing beside this spring, and the daughters of the townspeople are coming out to draw water. May it be that when I say to a girl, 'Please let down your jar that I may have a drink,' and she says, 'Drink, and I'll water your camels too'—let her be the one you have chosen for your servant Isaac. By this I will know that you have shown kindness to my master"* [establishing attitude and character test criteria].

The answer to prayer: *Before he had finished praying, Rebekah came out with her jar on her shoulder. She was the daughter of Bethuel son of Milcah, who was the wife of Abraham's brother Nahor. The girl was very beautiful, a virgin; no man had ever lain with her* [a critical criteria in Hebrew culture]. *She went down to the spring, filled her jar and came up again. The servant hurried to meet her and said, "Please give me a little water from your jar." "Drink, my lord," she said, and quickly lowered the jar to her hands and gave him a drink. After she had given him a drink, she said, "I'll*

[9] "Hebraic Insights -- Messages Exploring the Hebrew Roots of Christian Faith", Chapter #78, August 2011 by Yosef Brusherd

draw water for your camels too, until they have finished drinking" [answered prayer and confirmation]. *So she quickly emptied her jar into the trough, ran back to the well to draw more water, and drew enough for all his camels* [she's hospitable, and a good, strong worker too!] …

Propose because she's the one: *When the camels had finished drinking, the man took out a gold nose ring weighing a beka and two gold bracelets weighing ten shekels* [engagement or friendship ring]. *Then he asked, "Whose daughter are you? Please tell me, is there room in your father's house for us to spend the night?"* [they have to ask her dad]. *She answered him, "I am the daughter of Bethuel, the son that Milcah bore to Nahor."* … *Then the man … worshiped the LORD, saying, "The Lord … has led me … to the house of my master's relatives"* (NIV).

She passes the "good family test" and the family approves: *"Now if you will show kindness and faithfulness to my master, tell me; and if not, tell me, so I may know which way to turn"*

Asking permission from bride's father/family: *Laban and Bethuel answered, "This is from the LORD; we can say nothing to you one way or the other. Here is Rebekah; take her and go* [giving away the bride], *and let her become the wife of your master's son, as the LORD has directed"* [God is the arranger]. *When Abraham's servant heard what they said, he bowed down to the ground before the LORD* [thankfulness].

The engagement ring or symbol: *Then the servant brought out gold and silver jewelry and articles of clothing and gave them to Rebekah; he also gave costly gifts to her brother and to her mother* [dowry?].

An engagement party: *Then he and the men who were with him ate and drank and spent the night there…*

The bride still has to say "Yes" to the proposal: *Then they said, "Let's call the girl and ask her about it." … "Will you go with this man?" "I will go," she said* [bride has to say yes]. *So they sent their sister Rebekah on her way* [to the groom's family] …

A blessing from the family: *And they blessed Rebekah and said to her, "Our sister, may you increase to thousands upon thousands; may your offspring possess the gates of their enemies"* [family said good-bye and blessed her, prophetically!] … *So the servant took Rebekah and left.*

The bride goes [up the aisle] to the waiting groom: *Now Isaac ... went out to the field ... as he looked up, he saw camels approaching. Rebekah also looked up and saw Isaac. She ... asked the servant, "Who is that man in the field coming to meet us?" "He is my master," the servant answered. So* she took her veil and covered herself [not to see each other until the wedding day]. *Then the servant told Isaac all he had done.*

The wedding: *Isaac brought her into the tent of his mother Sarah, and he married Rebekah* [simply by consummating the marriage and living together in the Father's house]. *So she became his wife, and he loved her...* (NIV).

Definitions to consider
Engaged:
1. busy or occupied; involved: deeply engaged in conversation.

2. pledged to be married; betrothed: an engaged couple.

3. under engagement; pledged: an engaged contractor.

4. entered into conflict with: desperately engaged armies.

Betrothed
1. To promise to give in marriage:
was betrothed to a member of the royal family.

2. Archaic To promise to marry.
(set apart, consecrated, designated)

The Proposal
Biblically, who should ask who for her hand in Marriage?

Who chooses whom?

- Revelation 22:17 *The Spirit and the bride say, "Come!" And let him who hears say, "Come!" Whoever is thirsty, let him come; and whoever wishes, let him take the free gift of the water of life.*

- Deuteronomy 10:15-16 *Yet the LORD set his affection on your forefathers and loved them, and he chose you, their descendants, above all the nations, as it is today.*

- 1 Peter 2:*9 But you are a chosen people, ...* Who chose who?

- Ephesians 1:4-5 *For he chose us in him before the creation of the world to be holy and blameless in his sight. In love he predestined us to be adopted as his sons ...*

- 2 Thessalonians 2:13 *from the beginning God chose you ...*

- John 15:16 *You did not choose me, but I chose you and appointed you to go and bear fruit - fruit that will last.*

Who asks whom for the 'hand in marriage'? Who says 'Yes'?

Even though Abraham's servant had arranged for Rebekah to be wife of Isaac, the family of Rebekah required a decision or response of Rebekah. Genesis 24:57-60 *Then they (family) said, "Let's call the girl and ask her about it." So they called Rebekah and asked her, "Will you go with this man?"* "I will go," *she said. So they sent their sister Rebekah on her way, ... And they blessed Rebekah and said to her, "Our sister, may you increase to thousands upon thousands; may your offspring possess the gates of their enemies."*

In a similar way, the invitation to accept our Bridegroom requires us to say "Yes, I will walk with you, talk with you, tell you I am your own" as the song goes. It is biblical. Romans 10:9-10 says *That if you <u>confess with your mouth</u>, "Jesus is Lord," and <u>believe in your heart</u> that God raised him from the dead, you will be saved. Basically one is saying* "Yes Jesus, I want to marry you."

The Judeo/Christian church is somewhat unique in that both the bride and groom must 'consent' to the marriage. Whether their marriage is arranged by parents, or third parties, they cannot be forced to make a covenant against their wills. And God will not force us to a covenant against our will either.

Should he ask permission from the bride's father?

Here is a classic personal testimony showing how this might   work: My daughter, Beth, had been seeing Kirk, whom she met at church and I knew she was ready to say 'yes' if he ever got around to asking. I invited him to our businessmen's breakfast meeting with about 10 men. I asked someone at the head of the table to gather the 'prayer requests' from each of the men around the table. The turn finally got around to Kirk, sitting next to but before me in the sequence. Kirk started in his slow, deliberate, nervous tone which I'll paraphrase "I ... need ... to set up ... a meeting ... and find ... the (uh) correct words ... to say when . .. speaking to ... the father ... of the woman ... that I would ... like to ... spend the ... rest of my life with." Naturally the eyes of all the men were going back and forth between Kirk and me. Once again, I knew there was something special about the respect that Kirk had for authority, etiquette, and propriety; and that he would therefore make an excellent son-in-law. Yes, we had our meeting and the rest is marital history – they have provided Peggy and I with our 13th and 14th grandchildren, Charity and Faith.

Match made in heaven! -- God, our Father, knew who we needed. He <u>gave</u> permission for His son to marry us - John 3:16 *"For God so loved the world that <u>he gave his one and only Son</u>, that whoever believes in him shall not perish but <u>have eternal life</u>.*

The first marriage was arranged by God when he made Eve for Adam – God's perfect design for companionship. Now here is an interesting thought. Adam and Eve did not have a set liturgy, nor a church nor a synagogue nor a temple nor Bible Scriptures to reference, and obviously no customs to follow. All they had was their walks with God in the garden. What can we learn from this? Sounds like and idyllic service!

Here is another biblical example of the family giving permission to Abraham's servant to take Rebekah to be the wife of Isaac. (This is an example of an arranged marriage.) Genesis 24:51 *Here is Rebekah; take her and go, and let her become the wife of your master's son, as the Lord has directed."*

In John.17:6,9,24 Jesus prays to the Father in the actual 'Lord's Prayer'. He refers to us, His Bride-to-be, as "those you have given me". Thus the 'bride' is given by the Father to the Groom.

- *6 "I have revealed you to **those whom you gave me** out of the world. They were yours; you gave them to me and they have obeyed your word.*

- *9 I pray for them. I am not praying for the world, but for those **you have given me**, for they are yours.*

- *24 "Father, I want **those you have given me** to be with me where I am, and to see my glory, the glory you have given me because you loved me before the creation of the world.*

-

Where else can we, should we, receive counsel?

Peggy and I were blessed by a Marriage Encounter week-end on February 14, 1976. It must have been special because not that many dates are indelibly lodged in my mind. The purpose of the week-end was to enhance or improve our relationship, not necessarily to save it. While it meant much to us, the experience helps me appreciate the value of a program that came out of Marriage Encounter, namely Engagement Encounter. Young engaged couples attending this week-end experience have to deal with tough questions that they either forgot to ask or were afraid to ask during their dating or courting times. The tough questions like:

How many children are we planning to have?

Who will handle the checkbook and pay the bills?

What church will we attend? Will the children attend?

Where will we spend Thanksgiving and Christmas?

After dealing with these and a barrage of similar questions, a high percentage of the couples decide to just remain friends. That result represents prevention of broken marriages.

Many churches and ministers require some level of 'pre-marital counseling' before they will marry a couple. Again, to the credit of my son-in-law and daughter, Kirk and Beth, they sought the 'pre-marital counseling' from their pastor and also from our son, Beth's brother, who is a licensed minister. Believe me, her brother Joseph gave them a serious counseling session, checking out his future brother-in-law.

The role of 'Prayer'

If we are consulting parents, family, friends, match-makers, etc. would it not make sense to consult the Creator who put us here for a purpose? What were the Creator's first words to man? Genesis 1:28 *God blessed them and said to them, "Be fruitful and increase in number; …"*

The family should be praying for the pending marriage. Like Rebekah's family did as recorded in Genesis 24:60 *And they blessed Rebekah and said to her, "Our sister, may you increase to thousands upon thousands; may your offspring possess the gates of their enemies."* The family said goodbye and blessed her future.

That leads to the next topic. Shouldn't the announcement of a wedding be a reminder to us that the union needs and deserves prayer? Serious prayer? Yet, I cannot recall ever hearing of a pending wedding being listed on a prayer list. Many marriages are listed as needing prayer after issues arise. What's wrong with that picture!?!?

Should the engaged couple be praying for one another? Jesus, the Groom, prayed for His bride in John 17: 24 *"Father, I want **those you have given me** to be with me where I am, and to see my* *glory, the glory you have given me because you loved me before the creation of the world."*

And the bride-to-be should be praying for the groom, or Groom.

The 'Dowry'

Perhaps you've heard the story of Johnny Lingo, a man who lived in the South Pacific. The islanders all spoke highly of him. He was strong, good-looking, and very intelligent. But when it came time for him to find a wife, people shook their heads in disbelief. The woman Johnny chose was plain, skinny, and walked with her shoulders hunched and her head down. She was very hesitant and shy. She was also a bit older than the other married women in the village, which did nothing for her value. But this man loved her.

What surprised everyone most was Johnny's offer. In order to obtain a wife, one paid for her by giving her father cows. Four to six cows was considered a high price. The other villagers thought he might pay two or even three cows at the most. But he gave ten cows for her!! Everyone chuckled about it, since they believed his father-in-law put one over on him. Some thought it was a mistake.

Several months after the wedding, a visitor from the United States came to the Islands to trade, and heard the story of Johnny Lingo and his ten-cow wife. Upon meeting Johnny and his wife the visitor was totally taken aback, since this wasn't a shy, plain, and hesitant woman, but one who was beautiful, poised, and confident. The visitor asked about this transformation, and Johnny Lingo's response was very simple. "I wanted a ten-cow woman, and when I paid that for her and treated her in that fashion, she began to believe that she was a ten-cow woman. She discovered she was worth more than any other woman in the islands. And what matters most is what a woman thinks of herself."

Dowry - definitions:

Biblical bride price – מֹהַר, "mohar" in Hebrew, is the price paid for a wife. It is a nuptial present; some gift, as a sum of money, which the bridegroom offers to the father of his bride as a satisfaction before he can receive her. Jacob had no dowry to give for his wife, but he gave his services as described in Genesis 29:18; 30:20; 34:12. There are very interesting examples in Exodus 22:17 (price for seducing but not marrying a virgin) and in 1 Samuel. 18:25 (Saul required David to pay with the flesh of Philistines).

Traditional -- Money, property, or material goods that a bride's family gives to the bridegroom or his family at the time of the wedding. In many cultures, the dowry not only helps to cement the relationship between the bride and groom's families but also serves to reinforce traditional family roles and gender roles.

It is interesting to note that the "10 cow wife" story and the biblical definition is the opposite of the current, traditional definition. The biblical significance probably has more to do with the daughter being classified as property/chattel in the Eastern culture and therefore there is a need for reimbursement or purchase payment by the one who will be taking a worker out of the family.

Our story of Abraham portrays the biblical principle of giving gifts, sometimes confused with the Dowry. Genesis 24:51-53 *Here is Rebekah; take her and go, and let her become the wife of your master's son, as the LORD has directed." 52 When Abraham's servant heard what they said, he bowed down to the ground before the LORD. 53 Then the servant brought out gold and silver jewelry and articles of clothing and gave them to Rebekah; he also gave costly gifts to her brother and to her mother.*

In the New Testament we find that the Father and the Son have put up a deposit guaranteeing the marriage that is to come. *Now it is God who has made us for this very purpose and has given us the Spirit as a deposit, guaranteeing what is to come.* 2 Corinthians 5:5. The deposit of the Holy Spirit is evidence of His claim on us. And He will claim His property when He returns. He already paid the full price.

Point to ponder

What price did Jesus pay for His bride?

The 'Engagement Ring'

Remember that Abraham's servant conveyed the intentions of his master with a ring. Genesis24:47 *Then I put the ring in her nose and the bracelets on her arms.*

When God made a covenant with Moses to make the Israelite nation His People, he used a very lasting sign in the form of a ring. In Genesis 17:11-12 (God to Moses) *You are to undergo circumcision, and it will be the sign of the covenant between me and you.* In the Old Testament the focus was on circumcision of the flesh; whereas the New Testament focus is on circumcision of the heart. Actually, circumcision of the heart was always God's intent.

- Deuteronomy 10:16-17 *Circumcise your hearts, therefore, and do not be stiff-necked any longer.*

- Deuteronomy 30:6 *The Lord your God will circumcise your hearts and the hearts of your descendants, so that you may love him with all your heart and with all your soul, and live.*

In ministering to men, there is a way to view circumcision that moves a man to righteous thinking. For a circumcised man, the semen (seed purposed for procreation) passes through a **ring of blood**. Therefore, man needs to be respectful and careful of where that seed goes and its purpose.

Also, in Genesis 41:41-42 a ring signified a covenant authority and relationship -- *So Pharaoh said to Joseph, "I hereby put you in charge of the whole land of Egypt." Then Pharaoh took his signet ring from his finger and put it on Joseph's finger.*

The ring was typically a 'signet ring' which simply meant that it was used for sealing or signing documents with all the authority of the owner. How much authority passes to the bride when she is wearing the 'wedding ring', or even the 'engagement' ring? When we discuss the Ketubah later, we will see that the relationship is much more contractual than we customarily view the engagement relationship in our Western culture.

Preparing their future home

In Eastern culture and Bible times, the groom would immediately start building a new house for the bride during the Betrothal period. Obviously that was what Jesus meant in John 14:2-3 *In my Father's house are many rooms.....I am going there to prepare a place for you. And if I go and prepare a place for you, I will come back and take you to be with me that you also may be where I am.*

Question – Who will carry you over the threshold?

Jesus referred to "Rooms in Father's house". The custom in biblical times was for bride and groom to start married life in the Father's house (tent) and in a room set off by a curtain in the Father's house. After a year the curtain is removed – time to move out and build your own. By that time the couple was expected to have a child and need the extra space.

The bride has to wait in anticipation of the day when the bridegroom will come. We see that same picture in 1 Thessalonians 4:16-17 *For the Lord himself will come down from heaven, with a loud command, with the voice of the archangel and with the trumpet call of God, and the dead in Christ will rise first. After that, we who are still alive and are left will be caught up together with them in the clouds to meet the Lord in the air. And so we will be with the Lord forever.*

The role of 'Romance'

Romance – During the 'engagement' period, I do not think we have to worry about the couple learning to be romantic.

The Engagement or Betrothal

Just so they don't get too romantic!

And you know what I mean.

Maybe that is why engaged couples need prayer?!?!

The 'Marriage Registry'

As soon as she is engaged, she is telling the world so; and telling all the good things about her groom; and telling her family and friends in which stores she is 'registered'.

Revelation 3:5 tells of those brides-to-be who are registered in the Book of Life, scheduled to be the Bride in the "Wedding Supper of the Lamb". *He who overcomes will, like them, be dressed in white. I will never blot out his name from the book of life, but will acknowledge his name before my Father and his angels.*

Should we consider the alternative? Revelation 20:15 *If anyone's name was not found written in the book of life, he was thrown into the lake of fire.*

The 'Announcement' or 'Banns' of marriage

I remember as a child, growing up in the Roman Catholic Church and hearing 'Banns of Marriage' announced each Sunday. I thought it was 'right', even at my tender age, that a pending marriage ought to be publicized, announced and even 'bragged' about.

Question - What does a young woman do when she gets engaged?

Answer - **SHE TELLS EVERYONE!!!**

Do you suppose we are to do likewise?

What is the intent of the command to us found in Mark 16:15? *"Go into all the world and preach the good news to all creation."*

Why get so excited? What's coming?

Remember, this is a Foreshadowing of the "Wedding Supper of the Lamb" Revelation 19:7-9 *Let us rejoice and be glad and give him glory! For the wedding of the Lamb has come, and his bride has made herself ready. Fine linen, bright and clean, was given her to wear." (Fine linen stands for the righteous acts of the saints.) Then the angel said to me, "Write: 'Blessed are those who are invited to the wedding supper of the Lamb!'" And he added, "These are the true words of God."*

And in Revelation 22:17 *The Spirit and the bride say, "Come!"*

When that bride-to-be announces to her friends that she is engaged, have you noticed how boastful and proud she is? She says things like: --
"He chose me!"
"He's rich; He's got a good job."
"He owns a house."
"He loves me!"
"He will provide for my future!"
"I want to live with him forever."
"And He will make a good father for my children."

Points to ponder

Are you engaged or betrothed to Jesus Christ?

Did you say 'yes' when the Holy Spirit asked you to live with Jesus forever?

What will you tell your friends about your Husband to be?

Did Jesus Christ, our Fiancé

Choose you?
Is he rich?
Will He provide you with a house?
Does He love you?
Will He provide for your future?
Do you want to live with Him forever?

Selecting the Wedding Party

Role of **'Best Man'?** In the Abraham and Isaac account, the Servant was sent to select or find the Bride, traditionally thought to be the Holy Spirit's role? Genesis 24:*2 He (Father Abraham) said to the <u>chief servant</u> (Type of the Holy Spirit) ... go to my country and my own relatives and <u>get a wife for my son</u> Isaac."* Did God send his Holy Spirit to call, woo and invite you, too?

Role of **'Maid of Honor'?** The word 'honor' is of interest. In biblical times, and as it should be now, the concern for an unmarried young virgin is to retain her honor. In biblical custom and Eastern cultures today the family does not want to deliver spoiled goods to the Groom. Rebekah's Maid of Honor is described in Genesis 24:59 *So they* (her family) *sent their sister Rebekah on her way, <u>along with her nurse</u> and Abraham's servant and his men.*

It is the Holy Spirit's role to minister to the bride and to get her ready and protect her on the journey, just as He does for us today. That is why Jesus said in John 14:26 *But the Counselor, the Holy Spirit, whom the Father will send in my name, will teach you all things and will remind you of everything I have said to you.*

The Bride and the Groom typically choose their respective best friend for this important role. Our Best Man and Maid of Honor have already been chosen. Hallelujah!

Invitations are sent out

Revelation 19:7-8 *Let us rejoice and be glad and give him glory! For the wedding of the Lamb has come...* Revelation 19:9 *'Blessed are those who are invited to the wedding supper of the Lamb!'* Revelation 22:17 *The Spirit and the bride say, "Come!" And let him who hears say, "Come!" Whoever is thirsty, let him come; and whoever wishes, let him take the free gift of the water of life.*

Announcements and invitations to the reception/banquet are traditionally sent out by the bride's family. We too should be inviting family, friends and all others to come to the wedding (of the Lamb). Matthew 22:8-9 *The wedding banquet is ready, but those I invited did not deserve to come. Go to the street corners and invite to the banquet anyone you find.*

The Ketubah (Contract)

While it was biblically initiated, the Ketubah has become a Jewish custom. The beauty of considering The Ketubah preparation recognizes the pre-marital decision, the effort, and all the considerations that solidify the marriage vows. The following comments were excerpted from Wikipedia, the free encyclopedia.

An illustration of a Ketubah:

A Ketubah (Hebrew: כתובה, "document"; pl. ketubot) is a Jewish prenuptial agreement. It is considered an integral part of a traditional Jewish marriage. It states that the husband commits to provide food, clothing and marital relations to his wife, and that he will pay a specified sum of money if he divorces her.

Historically, the rabbis in ancient times insisted on the marriage couple entering into the Ketubah as a protection for the wife. It acted as a replacement of the biblical dower or bride price, which was payable at the time of the marriage by the groom to the bride or her parents. The Ketubah became a mechanism whereby the amount due to the wife (the <u>dower</u>) came to be paid in the event of the cessation of marriage, either by the death of the husband or <u>divorce</u>. Another function performed by the Ketubah amount was to provide a disincentive for the husband contemplating <u>divorcing</u> his wife: he would need to have the amount to be able to pay to the wife. (The Rabbinic custom grew from the biblical commands in Exodus 22:16-17 and Deuteronomy 22:28-29)

<u>Role in Wedding Ceremony is critical</u>. The Ketubah is signed by two witnesses and traditionally read out under the huppa (a canopy of a Tallit). The honor of signing the Ketubah is often given to a close family friend or a distant relative. The two who sign it must be valid to witness such a contract, so they must be upstanding members of the religious community without close blood ties to either side. It is then handed to the bride for safekeeping.

<u>Design and Languages vary.</u> Contemporary ketubot have many different styles of language and designs, depending on the beliefs and traditions of the couple. Traditionally, the language of the Ketubah formalizes the various requirements by the <u>Torah</u> of a Jewish husband vis à vis his wife (e.g. giving her adequate resources for dress, and providing her with regular sexual intercourse), and stipulates the sum to be paid by him in case of divorce, generally considered the sum to support oneself financially for a full year. A traditional Ketubah is written in language, similar in tone to marriage vows, which stress the values on which they base their relationship and marriage (love, companionship, family, tradition, etc.).

<u>After Marriage</u> the Ketubah is sometimes a popular form of Jewish art, or <u>Judaica</u>, found in the home. Ketubot are often hung prominently in the home by the married couple as a daily reminder of their vows and responsibilities to each other. Ketubot have been made in a wide range of designs, usually following the tastes and styles of the era and region in which they are made. Many couples follow the Jewish tradition of hiddur mitzvah which calls for ceremonial objects such as the Ketubah to be made as beautiful as possible.

The betrothal status was, is, and maybe should still be much more contractual, respected and thought through. It took a writ of divorce to get out of a Ketubah in those days, and that is still true today in the Jewish and Muslim Eastern culture.

Question -- Would women today feel much more secure if there was the protection of a Ketubah over their marriage?

Has Jesus given us an unbreakable promise like a Ketubah guaranteeing our eventual wedding and marriage – to last forever, sharing His riches and His love for us?

Points to Ponder –

Is the Holy Spirit of the Almighty God, King of the Universe, calling you?

Is He inviting you to be His bride at the "Wedding Supper of the Lamb"?

What an honor!

How have you answered Him?

Are you excited enough to tell others about your future husband?

Chapter 4

The Wedding

Genesis 24:62-67 *Now Isaac had come from Beer Lahai Roi, for he was living in the Negev. He went out to the field one evening to meditate, and as he looked up, he saw camels approaching. Rebekah also looked up and saw Isaac. She got down from her camel and asked the servant, "Who is that man in the field coming to meet us?" "He is my master,"* the servant *answered. So she took her veil and covered herself.* [Not to see each other until the wedding] *Then the servant told Isaac all he had done. Isaac brought her into the tent of his mother Sarah, and he married Rebekah.* (Lived in Father's house) *So she became his wife, and he loved her...*

What are some familiar wedding traditions?

What happens in preparation for the wedding?

What happens at a wedding?

When is "The Big (Wedding) Day"?

In our Western culture the newlyweds make the arrangements and pick the day. However, biblically that is not the case, as portrayed in John 14:2-3 *In my Father's house are many rooms; if it were not so, I would have told you. I am going there to prepare a place for you. And if I go and prepare a place for you, I will come back and take you to be with me that you also may be where I am.*

BUT WHEN? Mathew 24:36-38 *"No one knows about that day or hour, not even the angels in heaven, nor the Son, but only the Father. As it was in the days of Noah, so it will be at the coming of the Son of Man.* And similarly in Mark 13:32-34 *"No one knows about that day or hour, not even the angels in heaven, nor the Son, but only the Father. Be on guard! Be alert! You do not know when that time will come.*

These scriptures make more sense when one understands the underlying culture of those days. What did Jesus mean when He said, in red letters, *"I am going there to prepare a place for you."* In Mid-eastern custom and biblical times, the groom went to the bride's house and after an accepted proposal, the groom returns to his father's house. There the groom adds a room to the father's tent or house for the groom's future family. When the father decides the room is ready, then and only then is the son, the groom, sent back to the bride's house to get her. Notice that only the Father knows when. Then there is a big procession with fanfare as he gets her and he brings her to his father's house. Incidentally, the groom is allowed a sheet or wall to separate their room from the rest of the family's space. What was Isaac and Rebekah's wedding ceremony? All we are told is *"Isaac brought her into the tent of his mother Sarah, and he married Rebekah"*. In God's eyes, the marriage was consummated behind the tent sheet.

Understanding the custom of those days may help us to better appreciate what the disciples heard when Jesus spoke those words in Matthew 25:1-10 *"At that time* (Last Days) *the kingdom of heaven will be like ten virgins who took their lamps and <u>went out to meet the bridegroom</u>. Five of them were foolish and five were wise. The foolish ones took their lamps but did not take any oil with them. The wise, however, took oil in* *jars along with their lamps. The <u>bridegroom was a long time in coming</u>, and they all became drowsy and fell asleep. "At midnight the cry rang out: 'Here's the bridegroom! Come out to meet him!' "Then all the virgins woke up and trimmed their lamps. The foolish ones said to the wise, 'Give us some of your oil; our lamps are going out.' "'No,' they replied, 'there may not be enough for both us and you. Instead, go to those who sell oil and buy some for yourselves.' "But while they were on their way to buy the oil, <u>the bridegroom arrived</u>. The virgins who were ready went in with him to the wedding banquet. And the door was shut.* From this we learn that once the bride enters the door is shut.

Luke 12:35-40 ... *like men waiting for their master ... in the second or third watch of the night... . 40 You also must be ready, because the Son of Man will come at an hour when you do not expect him."*

Revelation 3:3 " ... *and you will not know at what time I will come to you."*

Why So Many Witnesses and Guests?

The role of the guests and witnesses is not always appreciated at the wedding ceremony. In biblical times, the minister or priest or rabbi was not required. It was the resolution by the couple in front of the witnessing community that constituted the sacrament of fulfillment of marriage. And that is true in many cultures today. Note in the biblical account of Isaac and Rebekah that simply bringing her into the family's home was all it took to be married. Genesis 24:67 *Isaac brought her into the tent of his mother Sarah, and he married Rebekah. So she became his wife, and he loved her...*

Who will be our witness on that grand and glorious day? Multitudes in Heaven – Angels, Animals, Those who have gone before, fellow warriors ... according to Revelation 19:6-7 *Then I heard what sounded <u>like a great multitude</u>, like the roar of rushing waters and like loud peals of thunder, shouting: "Hallelujah! For our Lord God Almighty reigns. Let us rejoice and be glad and give him glory! For the wedding of the Lamb has come,.."*

Zephaniah 1:7 *Be silent before the Sovereign Lord, for the day of the Lord is near. The Lord has prepared a sacrifice; he has consecrated those he has invited.*

The gathering of Witnesses, Family and Friends is typically acknowledged by words like these -- "Dearly beloved, we are gathered together in the sight of God, and in the presence of family and friends to join together this man and this woman." What is the role of witnesses?

1. To witness - They came to witness, and listen. They witness the sincerity of the bride and groom.

2. To validate - A witness is called to court to testify what has happened, so family and friends see the ceremony and testify to others.

3. To celebrate - Family and friends come to rejoice in their happiness. Remember, Jesus attended a marriage ceremony as one of His first actions in ministry.

4. To uphold and pray for them - Family and friends attend and promise to support the couple as they walk with God.

5. To accept them into a Christian community - The new couple should begin in the church community, live in the church community, and serve in the church community.

Brides wear "Something Old, Something New, Something Borrowed, Something Blue"

This may be stretching the source of this popular custom, but could this refer to:

- Old testament
- New Testament
- Borrowed 'robe of righteousness'
- Blue heavenlies – our future home

What Color is her wedding gown?

Revelation 19:7-8 *for the wedding of the Lamb has come, and his bride has made herself ready. Fine linen, bright and clean, was given her to wear." (Fine linen stands for the righteous acts of the saints.)*

Remember, linen is white, which symbolizes purity. What groom is not looking for purity in his bride? Virginity is typically required in the Ketubah, as well as proof thereof! Why is purity so important in biblical and Judeo weddings?

Why the fuss over the bride's 'Wedding Clothes'?

Isaiah 61:10 *For he has clothed me with garments of salvation and arrayed me in a robe of righteousness, as a bridegroom adorns his head like a priest, and as a bride adorns herself with her jewels.*

And the bride should be aware of the warning from Matthew 22:12 *'how did you get in here without wedding clothes?'*

Tough Question – How can the story and circumstances of Joseph and Mary's marriage help couples who find her pregnant before the wedding day? But consider this answer, using a question as an answer – What is God's plan for the future of the family? Is He more concerned about the present, or the future? Remember, Satan wants us to look back; Jesus wants us to look forward to our future.

We are not advocating pre-marital sex, but we recognize a reality that does arise.

Rehearsal Dinner

Passover Seder – the first of God's commanded feasts is a rehearsal for our marriage; just as our lives are now a rehearsal for the important marriage for all of us. And by the way – God's commanded feast days like Passover, Shavuot (Pentecost), and Sukkot (Booths or Tabernacles) were not just Jewish Feast days.

They were and are God's Feast Days. Deuteronomy 16:16 *Three times a year all your men <u>must</u> appear before the Lord your God at the place he will choose: at the Feast of Unleavened Bread, the Feast of Weeks and the Feast of Tabernacles.* A study of these feast days reveals God's plan to draw all men unto Him for the Wedding Supper of the Lamb.

Let's look at what Jesus meant at the Seder (meal) at Passover when He was looking forward to the Wedding Supper of the Lamb. It says in Matthew 26:27-29 *Then he took the cup, gave thanks and offered it to them, saying, "Drink from it, all of you. This is my blood of the covenant, which is poured out for many for the forgiveness of sins. I tell you <u>I will not drink of this fruit of the vine from now on until that day when I drink it anew with you in my Father's kingdom."</u>* This seder (meal) recorded in the Gospels was a rehearsal for The Wedding Supper.

Father of the Groom pays for the dinner by custom. So, before the dinner, the father incurs the cost. Sounds like John 3:16?

Let's explore fourteen more customs

Can we find the biblical significance in each of these traditional customs?

Custom #1

Bride and Groom not to seeing each other before the Wedding

There is a period of separation and expectant waiting. Who says "He cannot see Her until the wedding begins"?

Remember Genesis 24:65 *"He is my master,"* the servant answered. *So she took her veil and <u>covered herself</u>.*

2 Corinthians 3:15-16 *Even to this day when Moses is read, a veil covers their hearts. 16 But whenever anyone turns to the Lord, the veil is taken away.*

Matthew 25:4-6 *The bridegroom was a long time in coming, and they all became drowsy and fell asleep. At midnight the cry rang out: 'Here's*

the bridegroom! Come out to meet him!'   And   1 Corinthians 15:52
In a twinkling ... Suddenly

John 14:2-3 *And if I go and prepare a place for you, I will come back and take you to be with me that you also may be where I am.*

Custom #2

The Processional Entrance!

As the bride goes down the aisle all eyes and attention are on the bride. It is interesting, that in biblical times, the groom was the center of attention. Matthew 25:1-6 *"At that time the kingdom of heaven will be like ten virgins who took their lamps and went out to meet the bridegroom. Five of them were foolish and five were wise. The foolish ones took their lamps but did not take any oil with them. The wise, however, took oil in jars along with their lamps. The bridegroom was a long time in coming, and they all became drowsy and fell asleep. At midnight the cry rang out: 'Here's the bridegroom! Come out to meet him!'"*

The bride was expected to wait patiently for the groom because he was preparing the homestead-to-be. Biblical custom and proof ? John 14:2-4 *In my Father's house are many rooms; if it were not so, I would have told you. I am going there to prepare a place for you. And if I go and prepare a place for you, I will come back and take you to be with me that you also may be where I am.*

Maybe we have a lesson to learn?! Our attention should also be on the groom, who is going to provide for the bride. **Biblically it is all about Him.** So why is the bride the center of attention? In biblical days the Groom was the honored one. For example in Song of Songs 3:11 *Come out, you daughters of Zion, and look at King Solomon wearing the crown, the crown with which his mother crowned him on the day of his wedding, the day his heart rejoiced.*   And in Matthew 22:1-2 *"The kingdom of heaven is like a king who prepared a wedding banquet for his son."*

This reminds me of a semi-serious lesson: There are three features in a wedding that are of real significance. First is the opening walk down the <u>aisle</u>. Then all the activity takes place around the <u>altar</u>. Meanwhile we have a <u>hymn</u> being sung in the background. These three features sum up the bride's attitude during the wedding – "I'll alter him."

No comment.

Custom #3

Giving of the bride (typically by the father)

Approval and support. "Who giveth this woman, to be married to this man?" The father typically answers, "Her mother and I do."

Question -- In a biblical sense, who is giving us to the Groom?
Scriptural Answers:

- In John 17:24 *Jesus prayed "Father, I want those <u>you have given me</u> to be with me where I am, and to see my glory, the glory you have given me because you loved me before the creation of the world.*

- And in the most familiar scripture reverence is John 3:16 *"For God so loved the world that <u>he gave</u> his one and only Son, ...*

As the father gives the bride to the groom, he typically joins the hands of the bride and groom – the power of the touch. After all, didn't Jesus come to earth to be in touch with mankind.

Custom #4

Preaching, Prayer and Advice

Let us review a sampling of the typical preaching and advising that the presiding minister (be it a Rabbi, Priest, Justice of the Peace, etc.) delivers in order to both admonish and encourage the couple just before the recitation of vows. It is sometimes hard to distinguish between the prayers, preaching and advice, but maybe that does not matter. Here are some typical messages:

Defining marriage – "Father God...you have created the universe, the heavens and the earth. You have made man and woman for one another. You have instituted the sacrament of marriage wherein man and woman might be joined to become one flesh. It is for this purpose that we come to witness the union of (groom) and (bride) in Holy matrimony and to share with them on this joyous occasion as they make their vows to each other and before you. We ask your Holy Spirit to bless and sanctify this marriage from this time forth. AMEN"

An example of the charge to the Bride and Groom – "Today is a significant day. It is a defining moment. It is one of the most defining days of your entire life. But as significant as today is, it is just the beginning of your marriage. The amount of investment that you make into the future days of your marriage will result in a lifetime dividends. I now charge you, (Groom), and you, (Bride), in the presence of God, to remember that true love and the faithful observance of your marriage vows are required for a successful marriage and the establishment of a happy and enduring home. Keep the solemn vows you are about to make. Live with tender consideration for each other and your marriage and your home will last and endure.

God, in His Word has much to say about the importance of the sacrament of marriage:

In Genesis - The LORD God said, "*It is not good for the man to be alone. I will make a helper suitable for him... .He took one of the man's ribs... Then the LORD God made a woman from the rib he had taken out of the man, and he brought her to the man. The man said, "This is now bone of my bones and flesh of my flesh; she shall be called 'woman,' for she was taken out of man.*" (not taken out of the head or the feet, but the 'Side' of man).

(*to the Groom*) – In Genesis 29 God's word gives us a perfect example of man's role in the marriage relationship in His portrayal of Jacob's love for Rachel. Verse 20 says "*So Jacob served seven years to get Rachel, but they seemed like only a few days to him because of his love for her.*"

Marriage is so respected by God that Jesus' first recorded miracle was   at   a   wedding.

(*to the Bride*) - Did you know that Mary the mother of Jesus gave us some excellent advice: Reading from John 2 *On the third day a wedding took place at Cana in Galilee.   When the wine was gone, Jesus' mother said to him, "They have no more wine."   Then, His mother said to the servants (referring to Jesus), "Do whatever he tells you.*"

By the way, you do have one more marriage to attend after this one. Remember when He said to us '*Blessed are those who are invited to the wedding supper of the Lamb!*'

Acknowledging that Marriage is viewed as both civil and religious. We must recognize the Laws of our state so the minister says – "By the power invested in me by the State of (Our State)." And we must also recognize God, "I pronounce you are husband and wife, in the name of the Father, the Son, and the Holy Spirit."

However, what the 'state' can put together, the 'state' can take apart. But Jesus said in Red Letters in Matthew 19:5-6 "*...a man will ... be united to his wife, and the two will become one flesh ... Therefore what God has joined together, let man not separate.*") Does this need further explanation?

A total commitment is required – "Leave father and mother and cleave only to her/him." In biblical custom, the word 'family' is defined as a husband and a wife; children are not required in order to have a 'family'. Interesting thought when we look at parents today doting on the children in order to be viewed as a 'family'.

History lesson – "In ancient times, weddings were some of the most anticipated events of a lifetime. It was understood that the union of a man and woman signified new life and represented God's love and passion for humanity. So today we all participate in the oldest ceremony known to mankind. The purpose for today remains the same as it has for thousands of years – two lives uniting to become one. Here are the words of Jesus Christ as recorded by the apostle Mark 10:6-9 *"... at the beginning of creation God 'made them male and female.' 'For this reason a man will leave his father and mother and be united to his wife, and the two will become one flesh.' So they are no longer two, but one. Therefore what God has joined together, let man not separate."*

What is a key difference between Courtship and Marriage? – "You have been courting each other for a number of months and spent all that time finding out how much alike you are. From this moment on, you will find out how different you are." How many couples married more than a few months know how true this is?

Here is sage marriage advice. Most couples prepare for the wedding ceremony, but give little preparation for marriage. The 'vows' are like the starting line of a race. Are they both prepared to 'run the race'?

Custom #5

The Vows

Marriage is – **"For better or for worse."** Christians understand that sin corrupts everything it touches, thus there will be problems in life.

- The house will need painting.
- The car will need a tune-up.
- The yard will need weeding and cutting.
- Etc. (How many more can you add?)
- The relationship will need constant attention.

Inevitable – **"In sickness and in health."** Our bodies will get sick. A husband will care for a wife with cancer and a wife will care for a husband who is disabled.

The glue of a marriage – **"To love and cherish."** The word cherish means, "precious, valuable, or worthy." Treat one another as the most valuable possession in life. Husbands remember, *"her price is far above rubies"* (Prov. 31:10). Does the word 'cherish' remind us of ten cows?

Marriage is forever - **"Till death do us part."** No matter what happens, your vow is your integrity. So, how long should the marriage last? Is there death in heaven while living with Jesus? Maybe that is why God said in Genesis 3:22 *"The man has now become like one of us, knowing good and evil. He must not be allowed to reach out his hand and take also from the tree of life and eat, and live forever."* So, which marriage will last forever. The one here on earth does have an ending, but the one in heaven is truly forever because there is no death in heaven. Unfortunately in today's world, and in the church, the marriage will last only as long as 'love' lasts, instead of as long as 'life' lasts.

Inseparable – **"*What God hath joined together, let no man put asunder.*"** Don't even think about it! This means don't let any outside influences destroy the "union." What can destroy a marriage? It is a long list of Satan's schemes -- relatives, lustful flirts, busybodies, do-gooders, etc.

Then the actual Vows – **"Do you ____, take ..."** serve another important purpose, especially if the couple processes the wording beforehand. Thinking through the vows begins to prepare us for the reality behind the individual vows. It should start to prepare the couple for the 'what ifs' of life.

Finally Agreement – to the vow::

| Woman agrees, | **"I will."** | or **"I do."** |
| Man agrees, | **"I will."** | or **"I do."** |

Presiding Minister makes a pronouncement, **"I now pronounce you – husband and wife ..."** or "Today, in God's eyes, two individuals have become one flesh. Two independent families have become one interdependent family. And as witnessed before God and this company, they have given and pledged their love to each other, and have declared the same, by the giving and receiving rings."

"I pronounce that they are now, husband and wife, in the name of the Father, and of the Son and of the Holy Spirit, Amen."

Point to Ponder

What do couples miss when they live together without getting married?

Custom #6

The Ring

In ancient times covenants were established between tribes. These covenants could only be broken by death. One of the symbols of a tribal covenant was a visible scar on the ruler or king's thumb. The scar told all who were concerned that this tribe was in covenant with another tribe. Three characteristics are recognized in the wedding ring:

1) Precious Metal - Gold. A precious metal that becomes more pure as it goes through the refining fire. A couple's love becomes more valuable as they go through pressures together, free of impurities

2) A diamond. Considered the hardest substance on earth, the most desired gem; the man desires her more than any others

3) Round. Unceasing. Unending -- We get our love from God who is eternal, i.e., He never began and will never end. Our love will be endless because it is from God

Traditional Ring Exchange

- By the Groom: "I give you this ring, as a symbol of my covenant before God. I choose you to be my wife, to have and to hold from this day forward for better or for worse, for richer or for poorer, in sickness and in health, to love and to cherish as long as we both shall live."

- By the Bride: "I give you this ring, as a symbol of my covenant before God. I choose you to be my husband, to have and to hold …"

- By the 'minister': "Let your care and protection of these rings, be a reminder that you are to protect and care for each other."

In our Western Culture, this 'wedding ring' is the true signet ring. It carries with it the full authority of the other party. They can now commit one another; even more so than was the case with the 'engagement ring' we discussed earlier.

Luke 15:22 *"But the father said to his servants, 'Quick! Bring the best robe and put it on him. Put a ring on his finger and sandals on his feet.'"* That ring totally restored the youngest son to a position of authority in the household with full signatory rights. And the rings are held and provided by the Best Man (the Holy Spirit).

Custom #7

Unity Candles

Not two but one. Two burning candles are used to light one new candle, and then the separate candles are extinguished. *"A man shall leave his father and his mother, and shall cleave unto his wife and they shall be one flesh"* (Gen. 2:24).

Custom #8

The Kiss

Symbol of a new union. "You may kiss your wife." This is a symbol of love and affection. Have you kissed Jesus Christ – with love and affection? You might recognize that the kiss is also the beginning of the act of consummation. We will discuss that in the 'Honeymoon' section.

Custom #9

First Communion together

Frequently, the couple wants to and does celebrate their first communion together as a part of the wedding ceremony?

Communion as part of the wedding ceremony comes from the Pesach or Passover feast; and stresses remembering the past and recognizing a foreshadowing for the future. Here are some scriptures pointing out the origins and spiritual significance of communion. Deuteronomy 16:1 *"Observe the month of Abib and celebrate the Passover of the LORD your God, because in the month of Abib he brought you out of Egypt by night."* Mathew 26:18-19 *He (Jesus) replied, "Go into the city to a certain man and tell him, 'The Teacher says: My appointed time is near. I am going to celebrate the Passover with my disciples at your house."'*

It is customary the for groom to drink the wine and offer it to the intended bride. If she drinks it also, then she has accepted a covenant relationship to be wed. This is a blood covenant which is why Paul quoted Jesus in 1 Corinthians 11:25-26 *"This cup is the new covenant in my blood; do this, whenever you drink it, in remembrance of me. For whenever you eat this bread and drink this cup, you proclaim the Lord's death until he comes."* This passage speaks also of fidelity in the relationship, thus Paul continued to address the issue of us drinking from the cup unworthily. Matthew 26:27-29 *Then he took the cup, gave thanks and offered it to them, saying, "Drink from it, all of you. This is my blood of the covenant, which is poured out for many for the forgiveness of sins. I tell you, I will not drink of this fruit of the vine from now on until that day when I drink it anew with you in my Father's kingdom."*

Let us see how the communion custom fits with God's Feast days as commanded by Him in the Torah, Pentateuch (first five books). These 'everlasting covenant feasts' are (1) 'rehearsals' for the final marriage; and (2) history lessons to prepare the bride and groom for the wedding and meeting the family. There are final invitations sent out in the New Testament. For example, at Jesus' Passover Seder (meal) there were four cups of wine, now only three. When Jesus drank from the fourth and last cup he said *"...will not drink again until ..."*

Jesus' words in Luke 22:17-18 *"Take this and divide it among you. For I tell you I will not drink again of the fruit of the vine until the kingdom of God comes."*

Custom #10

The Bride's takes on the Groom's name

"Let me be the first to present to you Mr. and Mrs. (*last name*)" *APPLAUSE*

The exchange of names has long been a Covenant marriage sign. The Hispanic culture adopts family names into their formal name when they marry.

God gave Abram a part of His name to confirm an everlasting covenant, which could almost be called a 'marriage covenant'. He gave one of His two Hei's (H's) from YHWH to Abram to become 'AbraHam', the other Hei he gave to Sara who became SaraH). Genesis 17:5-7 *No longer will you be called Abram; your name will be Abraham, for I have made you a father of many nations. I will make you very fruitful; I will make nations of you, and kings will come from you. I will establish my covenant as an everlasting covenant between me and you and your descendants after you for the generations to come, to be your God and the God of your descendants after you.*

The Wedding

Acts 11:26 - *...first called "Christians" in Antioch.* Thus, we Christians have taken on the name of 'Christ', the last name of the bridegroom.

Isaiah 62:2 *The nations will see your righteousness, and all kings your glory; you will be called by a new name that the mouth of the Lord will bestow.*

Revelation 3:12 *I will write on him the name of my God... and I will also write on him my new name.*

Let us ponder the significance of carrying someone's name. My wife has become fond and protective and possessive of my last name which she received on our wedding day. My sons, likewise carry on the name with pride and honor. This is something to think about if we are to be identified as Christians! And family honor is to be protected when you carry the family name.

Custom #11

The Reception...Feasting at the banqueting table

Where did Jesus perform His first miracle?   John 2:1-10 - Jesus' first miracle – ... invited to the wedding. When the wine was gone ... the master of the banquet tasted the water that had been turned into wine. Considering the importance of the 'marriage' theme in His Word, this seems to be more than a coincidence.

Did HE enjoy weddings?   150 gallons of wine!

Song of Solomon 2:4

♫ *He brought me into His banqueting table* ... *His banner over me is love.*
I am my beloved's and he is mine ... *His banner over me is love.*
He is the Shepherd and we are the sheep, ... *His banner over me is love.*
He is the Vine and we are the branches, ... *His banner over me is love.* ♫

Revelation 3:20 *Here I am! I stand at the door and knock. If anyone hears my voice and opens the door, I will come in **and eat with him**, and he with me.*

Small point to ponder

Are church pot-lucks and a prelude to the reception we will have with Him.

Custom #12

Proposing a toast

Jesus proposed a toast on Passover with His apostles, who represented all of us. In Matthew 26:27-29 *Then he took <u>the cup</u>, gave thanks and <u>offered</u> it to them, saying, "Drink from it, all of you. 28 This is my blood of the covenant, which is poured out for many for the forgiveness of sins. 29 I tell you, I will not drink of this fruit of the vine from now on <u>until that day when I drink it anew with you in my Father's kingdom</u>."* Our traditional communion liturgy is far more meaningful as we reflect on the significance of the wedding feast that Jesus promised.

Custom #13

The Groom carries bride over the threshold

Is this the promise to us that Our Lord anticipated in 2 Peter 3:13 *But in keeping with his promise we are looking forward to a new heaven and a new earth, the home of righteousness.* Could that be what Jesus was thinking when He spoke in red letters in John 14:2-4 *"In my Father's house are many rooms; if it were not so, I would have told you. I am going there to prepare a place for you. And if I go and prepare a place for you, I will come back <u>and take you to be with me</u> that you also may be where I am. You know the way to the place where I am going."*

What is that place going to be like that Jesus is preparing for us? In Revelation 22:1-5 He gave us a description of our future home with Him. *Then the angel showed me (John) the river of the water of life, as clear as crystal, flowing from the throne of God and of the Lamb down the middle of the great street of the city. On each side of the river stood the tree of life, bearing twelve crops of fruit, yielding its fruit every month. And the leaves of the tree are for the healing of the nations. No longer will there be any curse. The throne of God and of the Lamb will be in the city, and his servants will serve him. They will see his face, and his name will be on their foreheads. There will be no more night. They will not need the light of a lamp or the light of the sun, for the Lord God will give them light. And they will reign for ever and ever.*

I can't wait!

Custom #14

The Honeymoon, ultimate intimacy

The honeymoon is understood to take the newly married couple into a state of ultimate intimacy, beyond "touching", to "penetration"; to "becoming one in the flesh", to being at one with Him. In Song of Songs 5:1 *I have come into my garden, my sister, my bride; I have gathered my myrrh with my spice. I have eaten my honeycomb and my honey; I have drunk my wine and my milk. Eat, O friends, and drink; drink your fill, O lovers.*

The expression 'being <u>in</u> Christ' takes on new meaning as we think in terms of the ultimate level of 'intimacy'. For instance, consider these references:

Romans 6:23 *the gift of God is eternal life <u>in</u> Christ Jesus our Lord.*

Romans 12:5 *so <u>in</u> Christ we who are many form one body,*

1 Corinthians 1:30 *It is because of him that you are <u>in</u> Christ Jesus,*

1 Corinthians 6:17 ... *he who <u>unites</u> himself with the Lord is one with Him in spirit.*

2 Corinthians 5:17 *if anyone is <u>in</u> Christ, he is a new creation;*

Ephesians 2:13 *But now <u>in</u> Christ Jesus you who once were far away have been brought near*

Colossians 1:28-29 *so that we may present everyone perfect <u>in</u> Christ.*

Colossians 2:9-10 *For in Christ all the fullness of the Deity lives in bodily form, and you have been given fullness in Christ,*

Even before the honeymoon begins, the presiding minister typically references Genesis 2:24 ... *And they will become one in the flesh.*

Question – Does 'becoming one in the flesh' happen at the wedding or over time during the marriage? Every married couple knows the answer to that question. It takes a few years and then the two are finishing each other's sentences and life settles into a mutually workable pattern.

We are all looking forward to the day when we will be 'as one' in HIM, FINALLY and FOREVER.

Point to ponder – for men

How does it feel as a man to be a bride?

To be a wife?

Submitted?

Point to ponder – for both men and women

Let us look then at Ephesians 5:22-24 *Wives, submit to your husbands as to the Lord. For the husband is the head of the wife as Christ is the head of the church, his body, of which he is the Savior. Now as the church submits to Christ, so also wives should submit to their husbands in everything.*

Submitted?

Are you, man or woman, fully submitted

to the best Husband of all?

The Wedding

Chapter 5

The Marriage

"*Never let the sun go down on your anger***"**

This is the only message I remember from our pre-marital
counseling 50+ years ago.

Have I always obeyed it?

No! But, it always came to my remembrance during the
'blue' times.

And it bothered me every time I disobeyed that Godly advice.

Ephesians 4:26-27 *"In your anger do not sin": Do not let the sun go
down
while you are still angry, and do not give the devil a foothold.*

Marriage was, is and always will be God's ultimate plan

Marriage was God's idea from the beginning. Genesis 2:18-25 *The LORD God said, "It is not good for the man to be alone. I will make a helper suitable for him." ... But for Adam no suitable helper was found. So the LORD God caused the man to fall into a deep sleep; and while he was sleeping, he took one of the man's ribs and closed up the place with flesh. Then the LORD God made a woman from the rib he had taken out of the man, and he brought her to the man. The man said, "This is now bone of my bones and flesh of my flesh; she shall be called 'woman,' for she was taken out of man." For this reason a man will leave his father and mother and be united to his wife, and they will become one flesh. The man and his wife were both naked, and they felt no shame.*

Many 'self-help' books have been written on the topic of 'successful marriages' or some similar theme. Without trying to re-state all those bits of advice, let's consider a few topics that flow from the courtship, engagement, and wedding topics we have already covered.

Since we just discussed the Wedding itself, let's start the discussion of our married lives with –

How can we protect our vows?

- Time together, like when you first dated.
- Respect, like you expect when you want his/her affection.
- Best behavior, like you expect from the others.
- Pray together, the family that prays together, stays together.
- Appreciation, kindness goes a long way.
- Communication. Why did God give us two ears and one mouth?

- Think in eternal terms, for how long? 1 John 2:17…*the man who does the will of God lives forever.*

- Promise to Love, Honor & Obey FOREVER 2 Corinthians 11:2 *I promised you to one husband, to Christ, so that I might present you as a pure virgin to him.*

At some point in life we probably said "I believe in my heart and I confess with my mouth that Jesus Christ is Lord of my life" or similar words. Thus we have vowed to make Him Lord of our lives. Let's consider the parallel between working to preserve our marriage here on earth with our pledged status with our Savior, Jesus Christ. After all, during the wedding ceremony our hearts certainly believed our love and devotion to our spouse and with our mouth we said "I do".

Responsibilities in Marriage

The honeymoon is over, so here are thoughts on what is involved to live out our ongoing responsibilities.

Marriage responsibilities are continual. It all began at the altar, but it does not end there.

- In the marriage relationship, I can never stop loving my wife and my wife can never stop loving me.

- In the marriage relationship, love is more than an emotion

- In the marriage relationship, love is more than a character trait

- In the marriage relationship, love is more than a feeling

- In the marriage relationship, love is a command

- In the marriage relationship, love is a four letter word; just like 'work' is a four letter word! *Our grandson led a youth group, and the key lesson he drove across to the young people is that 'Love' is a four-letter word; spelled "W-O-R-K".*

Marriage Is a Union, a Mutually Dependent Design

God designed two to become one flesh so it is too late to choose singleness after marriage. Here is what God understood:

- The closer the union, the more precious the union
- The closer the union, the stronger the union
- The closer the union, the more loyal the union
- The closer the union, the more secure the union

What this world needs is to get marriages surrendered to Christ and his power!

What is the difference between Union and Unity?

As we use the word 'union' in marriage discussions, I feel compelled to help define the difference between 'union' and 'unity'. (Remember the 'Unity Candle' custom?)

If you tie two cat's tails together you have a 'union'. But, do you have 'unity'?

Have you ever seen how sometimes after a 'wedding' we see a union, but the couple now faces the challenge of achieving 'unity'?

Open Communication & Intimacy

Personal testimony – On February 14th, 1976, Peggy and I went on a Marriage Encounter week-end and the question we were to process was "When in your marriage did you feel closest to one another?" I had no trouble answering the question. It was while we were building our first, and only, custom-built home. We had countless decisions to make – room sizes, colors, brick types, layout, door placements, trim, floor coverings, and on and on. So we were forced by the circumstance to spend a lot of time communicating.

It happened again when we moved to Europe in 1988 with many details to decide and mini-challenges to work through. So again we had to spend a lot of time communicating.

Let us keep this concept in balance. Marriage involves two uniquely different people learning to become one. Yet there is such a thing as getting too close. There is an old life-lesson involving 'how to keep a fire burning'. If the two logs are too far apart, the fire cools off and dies; and if the logs are too close together, they smother each other and the fire dies out – so, the objective is to know how to keep the logs just close enough.

For Peggy and I there was a practical example of this principle. A few years ago I had a job in which I worked out of the house (a real contrast to the traveling job). In our traditional Christmas letter we confessed to our friends that "Peggy married me 'for better or for worse' but not for lunch."

In perfect marriage communication nothing should be withheld from each other. And you definitely do not have the right to withhold affection and intimacy from a spouse. Apostle Paul recognized that in 1 Corinthians 7:2-6 ... *each man should have his own wife, and each woman her own husband. The husband should fulfill his marital duty to his wife, and likewise the wife to her husband. The wife's body does not belong to her alone but also to her husband. In the same way, the husband's body does not belong to him alone but also to his wife. Do not deprive each other except by mutual consent and for a time, so that you may devote yourselves to prayer. Then come together again so that Satan will not tempt you because of your lack of self-control.*

Closeness should not be used as a weapon; intimacy is not a bargaining tool. But closeness and intimacy are powerful forces against the immorality of this world! The relationship of marriage is so important to God that the closeness and intimacy is only to be broken by a devotion to prayer/fasting – a concentrated effort to seek the mind and will of God.

But even then, stipulations were placed.

- Mutual consent – if God were going to talk to one spouse about an issue, he would talk to both about the issue
- Specific Purpose
- Specific time

Immorality of the world is a powerful force and Satan knows he has the opportunity to affect the marriage, by affecting the intimacy of the marriage. Remember that sexual immorality changes us internally - at the heart level where Jesus is supposed to be residing!

The ultimate intimacy in a prophetically biblical sense occurred when Jesus was hung on the cross. He is typically portrayed wearing a loin cloth for modesty sake, and we sing a song "On a hill far away ...". To fully appreciate His crucifixion, here are two points to consider:

(1) He was crucified at the Damascus gate, still to this day the busiest gate in the city of Jerusalem, where the Romans figured He would receive the largest audience, and

(2) He was actually naked on the cross. By religious custom of the times, the only one who was to see a Jewish man's nakedness was his wife, or bride. Thus unknowingly a prophetic message was accomplished – the bride of Christ, the public-at-large, viewed their Bridegroom.

Marriage Is A Gift

Marriage and singleness are gifts from God, not a weighing of benefits. His Holy Spirit is here to equip us all to live married, and all are not equipped to live as singles.

Here is a Marriage Parable to ponder.[10]

---

[10] source unknown

I BROUGHT 3 KEYS TO MY HOME
A Gate, a Deadbolt and a Doorknob

Key I – Build it on Jesus   Since God created marriage then it is only right that you build your marriage on the solid rock of His son Jesus Christ. Jesus said in Matthew 7:24-27 *"Therefore everyone who hears these words of mine and puts them into practice is like a wise man who built his house on the rock. The rain came down, the streams rose, and the winds blew and beat against that house; yet it did not fall, because it had its foundation on the rock. But everyone who hears these words of mine and does not put them into practice is like a foolish man who built his house on sand. The rain came down, the streams rose, and the winds blew and beat against that house, and it fell with a great crash."*

I know that Jesus is your Rock. The rain/wind are trials of life – and they will come. But knowing that your marriage is founded on Jesus the Solid Rock, insures that it CAN withstand the storms that will come.

Key II – Healthy communication   Communication to a marriage is like fresh air to a body or oxygen to a flame. Without it your relationship will slowly suffocate. Nations go to war when communication breaks down. Cultures are divided when there is no clear dialogue. Jesus said it best in Mathew 12:25 *"... every city or household divided against itself will not stand."* Communication lines can clog quickly and the "air" supply will disappear before you know it. So to keep those lines open let's listen to what it says in Ephesians 4:26-27 *"In your anger do not sin":* *Do not let the sun go down while you are still angry, and do not give the devil a foothold.*

These call for two good ways to keep those communication lines open:

1. Be quick to forgive

2. Resolve anger on the same day

During an interview with a couple that had been married 80 years, they were asked how they did it? The first thing they said, "We talk through everything..." They understood the key of healthy communication.

> **Key III – Genuine Love.** Bible says in 1 Corinthians 13:4-8 *Love is patient, love is kind. It does not envy, it does not boast, it is not proud. It is not rude, it is not self-seeking, it is not easily angered, it keeps no record of wrongs. Love does not delight in evil but rejoices with the truth. It always protects, always trusts, always hopes, always perseveres. Love never fails...*
>
> Maybe we should all do a periodic "love test"?
>
> **THESE 3 KEYS UNLOCK A HOME THAT CAN LAST A LIFETIME.**

He Must Love; She Must Respect. Why?

Like many other married couples and those in ministry, we have traditionally heard that 'Love' and 'Communication' are the keys to happy marriages. Dr. Emerson Eggerichs' book entitled "LOVE and RESPECT"[11] identifies the missing ingredient in our traditional thinking. The importance of 'respect' in the marriage is revealed in the author's marketing blurb for the book.

Discover the single greatest secret to a successful marriage. Psychological studies affirm it, and the Bible has been saying it for ages. Cracking the communication code between husband and wife involves understanding one thing: that <u>unconditional respect is as powerful for him as unconditional love is for her</u>. It's the secret to marriage that every couple seeks, and yet few couples ever find.

The Secret?   He must Love her;   She must Respect Him

A similar biblical principle – Jesus loves us; We are to respect Him.

While we will not dwell in detail on the importance of 'respect', I strongly recommend Dr. Emerson Eggerichs' book as

---

[11] Eggerichs, Dr. Emerson *Love and Respect - The Love She Most Desires; The Respect He Desperately Needs.* Focus on the Family, 2004.

the best one I have found with the potential to save marriages.[12] His basic biblical foundation is based on the fact that Paul never told a woman to <u>love</u> her husband, and he never told the man to <u>respect</u> his wife. You do not have to tell someone to do something they do as part of their nature. Paul focuses on telling us what we need to do that is not natural for us to do. This little revelation is key to understanding that God made man and woman to be different, and therefore have different needs. Paul said it in Ephesians 5:33 *However, each one of you also <u>must love his wife</u> as he loves himself, and the <u>wife must respect her husband</u>.* Note the use of the word 'must'. I wonder why it says 'must'? Read the book!

Sources of Great Joy

Ecclesiastes 8:14-15 *So I commend the enjoyment of life, because nothing is better for a man under the sun than to eat and drink and be glad. Then joy will accompany him in his work all the days of the life God has given him under the sun.*

Children, a natural by-product of marriage, are a delight. Remember what the angel of the Lord said to Zechariah in Luke 1:13-15 *"... Your wife will bear you a son, ... He will be a joy and delight to you, and many will rejoice because of his birth, for he will be great in the sight of the Lord...".* Even angels know that children are a source of great joy. Do you think Our Father feels the same way about you? His child?

Although there will be times of great trials in any marriage relationship, consider what we were told by James 1:2-5 *Consider it pure joy, my brothers, whenever you face trials of many kinds, because you know that the testing of your faith develops perseverance. Perseverance must finish its work so that you may be mature and complete, not lacking anything.*

---

[12] The author knows of at least six marriages salvaged by sharing these teachings.

A Christ like relationship

The basis for successful marriage is principled, Christ-like love, not feelings. The apostle Paul was very direct and did not reference 'feelings' when he laid out the basis for a Christ-like husband and wife relationship. Ephesians 5:21-33 *Submit to one another out of reverence for Christ. Wives, submit to your husbands as to the Lord. For the husband is the head of the wife as Christ is the head of the church, his body, of which he is the Savior. Now as the church submits to Christ, so also wives should submit to their husbands in everything. Husbands, love your wives, just as Christ loved the church and gave himself up for her to make her holy, cleansing her by the washing with water through the word, and to present her to himself as a radiant church, without stain or wrinkle or any other blemish, but holy and blameless. In this same way, husbands ought to love their wives as their own bodies. He who loves his wife loves himself. After all, no one ever hated his own body, but he feeds and cares for it, just as Christ does the church – for we are members of his body. "For this reason a man will leave his father and mother and be united to his wife, and the two will become one flesh." This is a profound mystery - but I am talking about Christ and the church. However, each one of you also <u>must love his wife</u> as he loves himself, and the <u>wife must respect her husband</u>.*

Marital Fidelity

I heard a parable on this topic recently. Imagine having welcomed a spouse back from months or years of prostitution. She (or he) has collected trinkets from her lovers as memorials to them but now has long forgotten their original meanings. In the most intimate bedroom times she comes with those very trinkets around her neck saying, 'with these I show my love to you' (cf. Ex.32: 1 – 6). In Christian Theological terms, this is called "synchronism" (idolatry mixed in as "godly"). Finally, I would also like to come straight back to Hosea, who was God's sign of great mercy toward His people. He knows that His bride is innocent in heart and naïve toward so much of 'what happened to get us here'. "Hosea" shows us that He loves His bride far more than He hates "synchronism".

He only desires that we do not presume upon His grace any form of a license to sin.

Here are some verses that confirm what is already generally accepted:

- Malachi 2:13-15 *Another thing you do: You flood the LORD's altar with tears. You weep and wail because he no longer pays attention to your offerings or accepts them with pleasure from your hands. You ask, "Why?" It is because the LORD is acting as the witness between you and the wife of your youth, because you have broken faith with her, though she is your partner, the wife of your marriage covenant. Has not [the LORD] made them one? In flesh and spirit they are his. And why one? Because he was seeking godly offspring. So guard yourself in your spirit, and do not break faith with the wife of your youth.*

- Hebrews 13:4 *Marriage should be honored by all, and the marriage bed kept pure, for God will judge the adulterer and all the sexually immoral.*

- Fidelity is stressed in Deuteronomy 6:5 *Love the LORD your God with all your heart and with all your soul and with all your strength.*

- Revelation 3:11 *I am coming soon. Hold on to what you have, so that no one will take your crown.*

So ... to have Godly offspring, do not break faith with the wife of your youth. This leads to the next topic – how to raise Godly children.

What is the Best Environment For Raising Children?

Ephesians 6:1-4 *Children, obey your parents in the Lord, for this is right. "Honor your father and mother" - which is the first commandment with a promise - "that it may go well with you and that you may enjoy long life on the earth." Fathers, do not exasperate your children; instead, bring them up in the training and instruction of the Lord.*

Luke 13:34-35 *"O Jerusalem, Jerusalem, you who kill the prophets and stone those sent to you, how often I have longed to gather your children together, as a hen gathers her chicks under her wings, but you were not willing! Look, your house is left to you desolate. I tell you, you will not see me again until you say, 'Blessed is he who comes in the name of the Lord.'"*

One day I asked the pastor of the Catholic Church I was attending "Why don't we have a youth group in our church?" His answer revealed to me, amongst other learnings, that good pastors are guided by a sound mission plan and strategy. Pastor Bill's response was "We are focused on helping couples to have a healthy relationship with each other; and thus the children will be okay." And I must note that the church was heavily involved in Marriage Encounters and Engagement Encounter week-ends on which the couple spent three days learning to process tough questions and thus established life-long healthy relationships. Does that work? Peggy and I had our Marriage Encounter on February 14, 1976. I don't remember many dates in my life, but that one I do remember. We would not have celebrated our 50th anniversary if it were not for that week-end.

How does that relate to raising children? With a lot of luck and even more help from the Lord, all of our six children, the five spouses and all of the fourteen grandchildren that are of age are serving the Lord. In fact, they are all active in their churches and two of the families are on or going into full-time foreign missions work (foreign – meaning out of the country where we cannot visit them as often as we would like.)

Let me tie a few principles together here. Peggy respected me despite my bad habits – one of which was workcoholism (out of town Sunday night to Friday night while the children were in formative years). However, Peggy spoke positively to them about my love for my job, about the accomplishment, and did not degrade me for being away. As a result, all six children have an excellent work ethic. We have witnessed examples of wives speaking disparagingly of the fathers work and the father complaining about his work environment. That negativity and lack of mutual husband/wife support has resulted in children getting in serious trouble as a way of avoiding 'getting a job and going to work like dad did'. The pictorial example I use is of a high-school student approaching graduation. He thinks, do I want to go to work and have a miserable life like dad's, or should I take part in a drug deal and get my down payment on a Corvette? This decision is a no-brainer from that teen-ager's perspective.

Thus I rest my case – a healthy, Godly relationship between the parents is the best environment for raising children.

Family Education

The topic of Education seems to be interpreted as synonymous with the school system for children. Adults tend to feel they are already educated, unless they need trade skills to earn a living or a so-called 'better living'.

Therefore, one's education tends to end when one completes the formal program of grammar, high and possibly college education. The key words in that sentence are "tends to". Maybe education continues in areas of trades, news, weather, celebrities and other current events. But we should be addressing what is considered life's true education in matters of religion, history, literature, morality, philosophy, and maybe even, Bible study sometimes. (Please note the sarcasm) True education is religious teaching. Let's recognize that humanism as a religion just as Judaic - Christianity is a religion. So Christians ought to be concerned about the 'religion' that they received, and should still be receiving from their respective church fellowship. And realize their children receive religious education if they are attending the public education system.

Here are three paragraphs from *Hebraic Insights #47 What Were They Devoted To?—Learning*.[13]

---

[13] "*Hebraic Insights -- Messages Exploring the Hebrew Roots of Christian Faith*", Insight #47, August 2011 by Yosef Brusherd

1. It started in childhood. Children at about the age of five would start to learn and memorize the Torah, starting with Leviticus in order to learn what is righteous and holy, before learning anything else. And honey was fed in the initial reading session so the *word became as sweet as honey* (Ps119:103). By the time the boy was twelve, he was trying to memorize major portions of the Torah. Then at age thirteen, the boy would celebrate his bar mitzvah and be accepted as a man in the community. Incidentally, it is not surprising that Jesus was teaching at the temple at the age of twelve. Was that part of His bar mitzvah service in which the young man preaches to the community? Decision time would come at about age fifteen, when thee young man is either chosen to learn a trade or accepted to continue studying and memorizing the rest of the TaNaK. The age of thirty was the typical rabbinical ordination. Remember that Jesus was ordained, commissioned, by baptism (or mikvah) in the Jordan at about that age. But the learning culture continued for all men till their dying day.

2. Teaching was and still is the father's responsibility. Mother helped, but there was no public school. And a child that did not learn the law and also a trade was a disgrace to the father (and to his Heavenly Father). The center of education was the home. They used text-people, not textbooks. As the father and mother worked around the house, the children would be taught object lessons. Deuteronomy 6:6–9 prescribes the curriculum:

These words, which I am ordering you today, are to be on your heart; and you are to teach them carefully to your children. You are to talk about them when you sit at home, when you are traveling on the road, when you lie down and when you get up. Tie them on your hand as a sign, put them at the front of a headband around your forehead, and write them on the door-frames of your house and on your gates (CJB).

Homeschooling is not new; and observing diligent homeschooling parent–child interaction awakens one to the advantages of learning to capture teaching moments in daily life.

3. Education was supplemented by priests, prophets, and wise men. Priests were the custodians and expounders of the law (Dt. 31:9–13). Prophets championed moral righteousness and social justice. Wise men were respected for the Hebrew wisdom.

The Marriage

Biblically, the education of children is the responsibility of the parents and family and the church. Hitler and the development of the corrupt Third Reich government represents a classic recent example of what happens when the children become wards of the state and then the state educates the children. And remember how Nebuchadnezzar 'converted' the Hebrew children that went into exile in Babylon? Daniel 1:3-4 *Then the king* (Nebuchadnezzar) *ordered ... his court officials, to bring in some of the Israelites from the royal family and the nobility— young men without any physical defect, handsome, showing aptitude for every kind of learning, well informed, quick to understand, and qualified to serve in the king's palace. He was to teach them the language and literature of the Babylonians.* Yes, the king's goal was to brainwash the young, potential, future leaders. So, if a child of your marriage is to be a future bright leader (every parent's goal) then you need to wash their brains with God's word and other sound teachings. The public schools are not using the right soap. You understand what I am saying!

What do the children watch on television and other entertainment media? That is their education. And for how many hours each day are they studying the worldly educational material?

What did our Lord require of us parents in His Word? Deuteronomy 6:6-9 *These commandments that I give you today are to be upon your hearts. Impress them on your children. Talk about them when you sit at home and when you walk along the road, when you lie down and when you get up. Tie them as symbols on your hands and bind them on your foreheads. Write them on the doorframes of your houses and on your gates.* He, Our Lord, expects us to be teaching the commandments (613 of them in Hebraic Tradition) to our children basically at all times, continuously, every waking hour, with many reminders. And it is the responsibility of the parents, especially the fathers! Let's not abdicate the responsibility to a public school system.

Traditional Public School education processes assume the mind is a blank slate and the educator's job is to fill it up with a given set of facts. However, God has endowed each person, Man, Woman and Child with unique giftings. Biblical education is designed to encourage the development of those unique giftings in each individual. Parents were given that responsibility by God in Proverbs 1:8 *Listen, my son, to your father's instruction and do not forsake your mother's teaching.*

In Gary DeMar's book God and Government, Vol. 3, Chapter 9[14] – Sovereignty and Education, he discusses these issues in extreme clarity. Summary statement – the biblical models for children's education are Home Schooling and Christian Schools in order of priority. If that is not doable, the responsibility for washing of the brains is still the parents. And, the parents need washing of the brains also, especially if watching typical 'entertainment' fare.

Point to ponder

If children are not to watch 'Adult only' entertainment, then why is it okay for adults to watch it?

Monogamy and Polygamy

It is well understood that in Old Testament biblical times the practice of Polygamy was quite common and accepted - multiple wives in parallel. In current times we have Polygamy - multiple wives serially. OUCH! God sees, or saw, all this and gave instructions to future kings that we should all take to heart. He instructed kings in Deuteronomy 17:16-17 *He must not take many wives, or his heart will be led astray. He must not accumulate large amounts of silver and gold.* Then in the New Testament, we are given direct advice in the criteria for candidates for leadership roles in the church. 1 Timothy 3:2 *Now the overseer must be above reproach, the husband of but one wife, ...* But interestingly and apparently also common - 1 Peter 3:7 *Husbands, in the same way be considerate as you live*

---

14 DeMar, Gary. God and Government – Vol. 3, The Restoration of the Republic. American Vision, Inc., Atlanta, GA, 2001

with your wives, and treat them with respect as the weaker partner and as heirs with you of the gracious gift of life, so that nothing will hinder your prayers.

Marital Satisfaction Factors:

In a survey of 3,000 American married women[15] 44% of respondents said they would say "I do" again, but 56% were not so sure. Why were they responding in the negative? Cheating and bickering were predominant answers. The survey indirectly showed it might be the woman's fault to some degree. To quote – "on the subject of how much women tell their best friends about their relationship, 44% said they reveal 'tons' to 'every intimate detail.' Is it possible these women are engaging in too much talk about their spouses and not enough talk with their spouses on important issues?" By contrast, in my personal experience hanging around with and in leadership roles ministering to men, I have NEVER heard a man seriously berating his wife. On the contrary, when men talk about their wives, they are supportive and at worst, will take the blame for any hint of inappropriate behavior on their wife's part. Need biblical support? Let us review a few from Proverbs 10:19 *When words are many, sin is not absent, but he who holds his tongue is wise.* And 12:18 *Reckless words pierce like a sword, but the tongue of the wise brings healing.* And 18:8 *The words of a gossip are like choice morsels; they go down to a man's inmost parts.* And repeated again in 26:22 *The words of a gossip are like choice morsels; they go down to a man's inmost parts.*

Divorce is Not an option

Unfortunately there is a whole set of humor built on the discord that occurs in marriages. A humorous example follows:

> *Marriage is like a deck of cards.*
>
> *In the beginning all you need is two hearts and a diamond.*
>
> *By the end, you wish you had a club and a spade.*

---

[15] Jennifer Christman's column *"If allowed do-overs, they'd say 'I don't'"*

I have heard of couples that resolved early in their marital process to never use the "D" word. And I have seen that resolution save some of those marriages. That is something to consider.

Divorce is rather misunderstood in our current Christian culture. Since the divorce rate is the same or worse among Christians, are we being taught correctly or is there a tendency for the church to avoid and thereby mis-teach the topic? With so many congregants divorced and re-married, the pastors and leaders have a difficult time preaching the way Jesus taught.

Question – What did Jesus teach about divorce? Surprisingly – Jesus did not forbid divorce. In Mathew 5:32 Jesus says *"But I tell you that anyone who divorces his wife, except for marital unfaithfulness, causes her to become an adulteress, and anyone who marries the divorced woman commits adultery."*

Notice what Jesus also said *"... anyone who marries the divorced woman commits adultery."* May I propose that last part is not stressed enough in church to discourage getting a divorce.

Let's summarize this topic by realizing that we do not want to break our marital relationship with Jesus and not be the bride at the Wedding Supper of the Bride. Even during the 'betrothal' period a broken relationship is breaking the Ketubah contract.

Point to ponder -

**Would the divorce rate among Christians diminish
if the party contemplating divorce was reminded
"Okay, but divorce ends your sex life."**

The Marriage

Chapter 6

Conclusion

He proposed to you!

What was, is and should be our answer?

His proposal to us

There is no question that Jesus has the 'marriage supper of the Lamb' in His heart throughout the entire Bible, indeed, throughout the entire plan of the triune Godhead, from day six when He created Man.

He, Jesus, has proposed to us. He has asked us to be his bride. When and if we say "Yes, Jesus Christ is my Lord" we have vowed to honor and obey Him as our Master. We said "Yes, I believe in my heart and I confess with my mouth that Jesus is my Lord." So according to 2 Peter 3:13 *But in keeping with his promise we are looking forward to a new heaven and a new earth, the home of righteousness.*

Since He is preparing the perfect new home, let us put our relatively petty and selfish things aside, love our spouse as we love our 'Groom to be' and let this be scriptural basis for living out this life. As a result, our lives, our marriages will be an inspiration and positive influence on (a) other married couples around us, (b) young people who are in various stages of contemplating marriage and most of all (c) our children – including all the children who are watching us.

In March of 2012 my wife of 52 years, Peggy, died after a series of prolonged health challenges. As friends and family proceeded past the casket for the final viewing at the funeral I said –

"You will notice that Peggy is not wearing our wedding ring. She has a new and perfect husband. And I am okay with that."

It is true, but it was not easy to say.

Action needed?

If you have never really accepted Jesus as your personal Savior, would you do it right now? Do not delay or put it off. If you would like to receive Christ by faith, pray this simple prayer in your heart:

> Dear Father, I know that I am separated from you, for I have sinned. I believe that Jesus Christ died on the cross and shed His blood for my sins, and I receive your forgiveness. I want to turn from my way and go your way.
>
> Lord Jesus, I now invite you into my heart as my personal Lord and Savior and I will follow and obey you as the Lord of my life...in Jesus' name...Amen.

If you prayed that prayer, God heard you and answered your prayer. I personally want to welcome you to the family of God. If this is the first time you prayed this prayer, please contact me at Yosef1@cox.net and tell us about your decision so that we can rejoice with you.

BIBLIOGRAPHY & related reference books

NIV *New International Version*
Colorado Springs: International Bible Society, 1984.

Brusherd, Joe, and Faith Ashley. *Our Hebraic Roots: A Twelve-Week Yeshiva*, 2007.

Brusherd, Joe a.k.a. Yosef. *Hebraic Insights – Messages Exploring the Hebrew Roots of Christian Faith*. iUniverse, 2011

DeMar, Gary. *God and Government* – *Vol. 3, The Restoration of the Republic*. American Vision, Inc., Atlanta, GA, 2001

Eggerichs, Dr. Emerson *Love and Respect - The Love She Most Desires; The Respect He Desperately Needs*. Focus on the Family, 2004.

Friedman, David. *They Loved the Torah: What Yeshua's First Followers Really Thought about the Law*. Clarksville, MD: Messianic Jewish Publishers, 2001.

Ingram, Chip. *Love, Sex, and Lasting Relationships.* Baker Books, Grand Rapids, MI 2003.

Johnson, Kurt. "*Greek Insights*." (weekly e-mails) 2009–2011.

Kasden, Barney. *God's Appointed Times: A Practical Guide for Understanding and Celebrating the Biblical Holidays*. Clarksville, MD: Messianic Jewish Publishers, 1993.

Sampson, Robin, and Linda Pierce. *A Family Guide to the Biblical Holidays*. Woodbridge, VA: Heart of Wisdom, 2001.

Sheldon, Charles M. *In His Steps*. Grand Rapids: Chosen Books, 1984.

Stevens, R. Paul & Gail. *Marriage* – *Learning from couples in scripture*. WaterBrook Press, Colorado Springs, CO, 1991.

Taylor, Kenneth N. *Almost 12:The Story of Sex*. 3rd ed. Wheaton, IL: Tyndale House, 1995.

Wilson, Marvin R. *Our Father Abraham: Jewish Roots of the Christian Faith*. Grand Rapids: Wm. B. Eerdmans 1989..

ABOUT THE AUTHOR

Contact Information

Joe "Yosef" Brusherd

710 Summit Loop

Rogers, AR 72756

Yosef1@cox.net

www.InsightsByYosef.com

Joe Brusherd's career included roles as CPA, international consultant, and vice-president in multiple companies. But one day in 1977, Joe Brusherd fell to his knees and said "Jesus Christ, you are real! I need to learn more about you." That was, is, and always will be his goal in life.

Since then he attended every Bible study possible, studied in several Bible colleges, and taught Sunday school classes in all churches of which he was a member. Joe led numerous men's ministries and Bible studies and developed (1) an in-depth survey of the Old Testament (his favorite topic), (2) outlines of Parashot (weekly Torah studies), and (3) a course curriculum called "Our Hebraic Roots," which became the introductory course in the yeshiva (school) in the messianic fellowship.

Although Joe was born again and baptized in the Holy Spirit in the Catholic Church, he has ministered in many distinctly different denominations: Assemblies of God, Filipino Assemblies of the First Born (as a licensed minister), Baptist, FourSquare, and more recently, in messianic fellowships. He started and led men's ministries in three distinctly different denominations: Assemblies of God, Filipino Assemblies of the First Born, and a messianic fellowship. A multidenominational background provides Joe with unique perspectives and insights.

As president of Full Gospel Business Men's chapters in California and Belgium, Joe lead large monthly dinner meetings and still leads a continuous schedule of weekly breakfast or lunch meetings worldwide. He has listened to hundreds of brothers from California Belgium, Honduras, and the Philippines share their testimonies.

This book, *Biblical Marriage*, was the first one drafted and includes many observations, testimonies, and teachings gleaned from personal experiences. Initial inspiration came from a teaching on the wedding supper of the Lamb. The initial distribution of the marriage book was limited to family and friends. However, family and friends comprise a large group since Joe and Peggy recently celebrated their fiftieth wedding anniversary, with six children, five of their spouses, and fourteen grandchildren, all of whom know, love, and serve the Lord.

Since drafting *Biblical Marriage*, Joe faithfully published a weekly series of e-mail messages entitled "Hebraic Insights" with inspiration and guidance from the Holy Spirit. During two years the distribution grew to over one hundred recipients, and these "Insights" were published recently as *Hebraic Insights – Message Exploring the Hebrew Roots of Christian Faith*, by Yosef. And he now publishes another weekly e-mail series referred to as "Hebraic Musings" which is available on request to – Yosef1@cox.net.

Joe is the first to admit that the best preparation for teaching comes from listening attentively to an assortment of Bible college classes, preparing Bible study and Sunday school lessons, and hearing three messages in a typical week, of a variety of denominations over the last thirty-two years. And frequently he listens to himself prepare and deliver the message of the week.

Proof

Made in the USA
Charleston, SC
16 May 2012